good enough
ISN'T
good enough

by Jack Cottrell

God's Wonderful Grace

Obtain a 40-page leader's guide to accompany this paperback.
Order number 1962 from Standard Publishing or your local
supplier.

New Life
BOOKS

A Division of Standard Publishing
Cincinnati, Ohio 45231
No. 40031

Other Bible versions used:
KJV—*King James Version* of 1611
NAS—*New American Standard Bible,* © 1963 by the Lockman Foundation.
RSV—*Revised Standard Version,* © 1946 and 1952.
ASV—*American Standard Version,* © 1929.

© 1976, The STANDARD PUBLISHING Co.
a division of Standex International Corp.
Chapter themes based on International Bible Lessons for Christian Teaching, © 1973 by the Lesson Committee.

Library of Congress Catalog No. 75-44590
ISBN 0-87239-060-8

Printed in U.S.A.   1976

Table of Contents

Introduction:
The Doctrines of
Salvation

The chapters in this book are based on selected passages from Galatians and Romans. They deal with such grand themes as justification by faith, law and grace, Christian freedom, reconciliation, the new birth, and assurance of salvation. There are no more exciting themes in all of Scripture!

Some folks are frightened by such words as justification, propitiation, and regeneration. This is unfortunate as well as unnecessary. It is unnecessary because they *can* be understood, though not without some effort in study. It is unfortunate because those who shy away from such "gems of Bible doctrine" (as one writer has put it) are robbing themselves of great pleasure and benefit.

We must learn to be more specific in the area of Bible doctrine. It may be sufficient in the beginning to understand simply that we are sinners, that Christ has died for our sins, and that we are now saved. But if this is all God wanted us to know, a couple of pages of revelation would have sufficed.

We have much, much more than this. The wells are deeper; the mines are much richer. Shall we not plunge into them? Shall we not learn the difference between law and grace? between the guilt of sin and the corruption of sin? between propitiation, redemption, and reconciliation? between justification and regeneration?

It is my personal conviction that one of the greatest needs of our churches today is to learn the difference between law and grace. Consequently an attempt has been made to carry the theme of grace throughout the book. Since the lesson themes were already predetermined, however, the attempt is not evenly successful. But it is my hope that individuals and study groups will be led to a deeper appreciation of God's wonderful grace, and that they will be motivated to pursue further study of the subject.

Chapter 1

100% Innocent

"Get right with God!"

This admonition confronts us occasionally from signs along country highways. It is really not bad advice. In fact, it is very good advice. What could be more important than being right with God?

The gospel of Jesus Christ speaks to this issue. The gospel—the *good news*—is that we *can* be right with God through faith in Jesus. Galatians 2:16 says that " a man is not justified by observing the law, but by faith in Jesus Christ."

In this chapter our goal is to understand what it means to be justified by faith.

I. What Is Faith?

Many persons find it difficult to accept the fact that we are justified by faith because they misunderstand the nature of faith. Thus our first task is to define faith.

Scripture Resource: Galatians 2:15, 16; 3:1-14

A. Faith is *Assent*

The faith which justifies contains two essential elements. The first of these is often called *assent*. Assent is an intellectual judgment, a belief that something is true. It is a judgment of the mind regarding the truth of a statement.

All of us are constantly called upon to exercise faith in this sense. "I believe that George Washington really crossed the Delaware River," says the student. "I believe that the stuff you are pumping into my gas tank really is gasoline," we say in effect to the service station attendant. "We believe that you are an honest person and a good credit risk," says the department store that issues us a credit card.

What causes a person to yield his assent to any such proposition? Basically we are compelled by the sufficiency of the evidence. We believe that something is true if the evidence is sufficient. Historical records, including the testimony of the eyewitnesses, are sufficient to convince us that Washington did cross the Delaware. We believe that clear fluid is gasoline because it looks and smells like it, and because nothing but gasoline has ever been known to come out of that pump. The department store issues a credit card only when it has received the evidence of our good credit performances in general.

Christian faith, justifying faith, includes such assent. "And without faith it is impossible to please God, because anyone who comes to him must believe that he exists and that he rewards those who earnestly seek him" (Hebrews 11:6). Martha of Bethany summarizes our faith in Christ thus: "I believe that you are the Christ, the Son of God, who was to come into the world" (John 11:27). The Apostle Paul adds that if you "believe in your heart that God raised him from the dead, you will be saved" (Romans 10:9).

These are just some of the statements that we believe are true. Why do we believe them? What compels our assent? Nothing less than the evidence. Jesus himself gave the basic evidence in the miracles He performed. (See Mark 2:1-12; John 2:11.) His own resurrection was the climactic evidence (Romans 1:4). Eyewitnesses have given us trustworthy testimony of these miraculous signs: "Jesus did many other miraculous signs in the presence of his disciples, which are not recorded in this book. But these are written that you may believe that Jesus is the Christ, the Son of God" (John 20:30-31).

Thus faith is first of all believing that these grand claims are true: that God loves us, that He gave His only begotten Son for us, that Jesus died for our sins, that He rose from the dead, that He will give us remission of sins and the gift of the Holy Spirit in Christian baptism, and many others.

But is it sufficient simply to believe that these things are true? Will a person be justified by merely accepting the truth of these statements? The answer is no. Even demons have this much faith, yet they are lost (James 2:19; Mark 1:24). Justifying faith is more than mere acceptance of the testimony as true.

B. Faith Is *Trust*

This leads us to the second element of faith, namely, *trust.* Trust is more than an intellectual judgment. It involves a commitment of the whole self. It is a decision of the will regarding surrender to a person. It is the surrender of yourself (or something in your power) into the control of someone else. It is thus an attitude of confidence in another person.

An everyday example of trust is hiring a babysitter to care for your children. In hiring a babysitter you are surrendering perhaps your most precious possession into the hands of someone else. Hence you want someone you can trust, someone you can have confidence in. Another example is going to a doctor. Since you are surrendering your life and health to his care, you want a doctor you can trust, one you can believe in.

This is the difference between assent and trust. Assent is believing *that* certain statements are true; trust is believing *in* a person. Justifying faith certainly includes trust, since it is believing *in* (or *on*) Jesus as Saviour. (See John 3:16; Acts 16:31.) It is a decision to commit your whole life to Jesus and His way. It is trusting yourself into His hands (2 Timothy 1:12).

An illustration which expresses very well the distinction between assent and trust is the story of the French tight-rope artist who performed some decades ago. One day, it is reported, he was giving an exhibition at Niagara Falls. He walked a rope strung across the gorge, doing all sorts of unusual and breath-taking stunts.

Finally he pushed a wheelbarrow across the rope. Returning to solid ground, he walked up to a small boy who was watching, spellbound. The acrobat was obviously a hero to the lad, so he asked him, "Young fellow, you think I'm pretty good on this rope, don't you?"

"Yes, sir!"

"You probably believe I can do just about anything on this rope, don't you?"

"Yes, sir! I believe you really can!"

"Do you believe that I could even put a person in this wheelbarrow and wheel him across the rope to the other side?"

"Indeed I do, sir!"

"All right. Hop in!"

But the boy, who had expressed his *assent* with such conviction, could not muster the personal *trust* required for that step. He refused to surrender himself into the acrobat's hands.

The faith which justifies us before God includes both assent and trust. We believe that Jesus is the Christ, the Son of God, and that he died for our sins and rose again. We believe his promise to forgive our sins and give us the gift of the Holy Spirit in Christian baptism (Acts 2:38).

10

Therefore we put our trust in him, committing our life to him as Lord. This continued trust and commitment is the faith which justifies us.

II. What Is Justification?

The gospel is that we are *justified* by faith. What does this mean? What does it mean to be justified?

To understand and appreciate justification, we must understand our predicament as sinners. Sin is basically a breaking of God's law (1 John 3:4). When we sin, we enter into a wrong and disastrous relationship to God and his law. We become guilty before the law, and stand under its penalty and condemnation. We exchange God's favor for His wrath. If we continue in this relationship of guilt, we will be condemned to hell forever.

We know we have sinned (Romans 3:23) and therefore stand guilty and condemned. But is there no hope? Is there not some way to get rid of this guilt and once more be in a right relationship to God and His law? Can we indeed "get right with God"?

A. Legal Pronouncement

The answer is yes! We can be *justified.* This is a legal term and refers to the verdict pronounced in a courtroom by a judge. To be justified means to be *pronounced "not guilty."* It means that God looks upon us, as guilty and sinful as we are, and declares us not guilty. He forgives us. He remits the punishment due to our sins. He takes the guilt away. He sets aside the penalty, the condemnation required by the law. He treat us just as if we had never sinned. Hallelujah!

How can God do this? He knows we are sinners, but He promises not to hold our sins against us. What enables God to hold back His wrath from us, to withhold the curse of the law from us? Only one thing: Jesus Christ has already suffered the full penalty of the law for us, in our place. "Christ redeemed us from the curse of the law by becoming a curse for us . . ." (Galatians 3:13). When He died on the cross, He was suffering in His body and spirit the eternal punishment due to every sinner.

B. Given Through Baptism

What, then, delivers us from this punishment? Our faith in Christ. We are truly "justified by His blood" (Romans 5:9), but only when we put our "faith in his blood" (Romans 3:25). This is how we are justified by faith. It is not just a general, vague faith in God's love and goodness. It is faith in Jesus Christ, faith that He has indeed "paid it all" through His suffering and death.

One very important point should not be overlooked. Even though we are justified *by* faith, we are not justified *as soon as* we have faith. Such a view, though held by many, is a very serious error. It confuses *means* with *occasion.* Faith is the means of justification, but according to the Bible, baptism is the occasion during which justification is given. Jesus has promised to meet us in Christian baptism and at that moment apply His blood to us for remission of sins (Acts 2:38; Romans 6:4-6; Colossians 2:12; Galatians 3:27). If we believe this promise, then we will meet Him there and be justified.

C. 100% Innocent

Being justified is something that happens to us immediately and completely. It does not come upon us gradually because it is not given in degrees. When God declares you "not guilty" in His sight, He means that from that moment you are considered one hundred percent innocent.

We should remember that this is what happens to the believer *now,* in this life, beginning with his baptism. We do not have to wait until the judgment day to be justified. We are justified now; we live now as justified persons, forgiven persons. We continue in this state of forgiveness as long as we maintain our justifying faith in Christ.

Being justified does not mean that we have no sin. It means rather that we have no condemnation. "Therefore, there is now no condemnation for those who are in Christ Jesus" (Romans 8:1). We trust in the blood of Christ; we trust that it covers our sins and absorbs their punishment. Therefore we live without fear of hell; we have "blessed assurance."

You can illustrate justification in this way. First, on a piece of white paper draw an outline of a human figure with blue or black ink. Then deface the figure by writing in the names of various sins with red ink. (This is our actual condition.) Finally, lay a piece of clear red cellophane or plastic over the whole drawing. What happens? The sins are "blotted out," and all that remains visible to our eyes is the original figure.

This is what happens when we are justified. We are laden with sins; but we are brought under the blood of Christ, which in a figure hides our sins from God's eyes. Thus He can declare us righteous. Through faith in Christ's blood, we are right with God.

No wonder "justification by faith" is good news, the very heart of the gospel. The more we know about it, the more we marvel at God's wisdom; the more we love Him for His love; the more we rest in peaceful confidence upon the work of Christ.

The chapters which follow will attempt to provide further insights into this great subject.

Chapter 2

Grace: More Than Fair

Justified by faith! Why is this such good news? What is so wonderful about it? We can answer this question fully only when we compare it with the alternative.

The alternative to justification by faith is justification by works. The gospel is not simply that we can be saved rather than lost. The good news is that we can be saved by *faith* rather than by works of law. (See Galatians 2:16; Romans 3:28; Ephesians 2:8-10.)

For instance, when Paul discusses the gospel in the book of Romans (see 1:16-17), his main concern is not the difference between sin and salvation. His primary purpose is to contrast the two possible ways of salvation: by grace through faith, or by law through works. Thus in theory there are two roads to God.

Paul's point, however, is that one of these roads (works of law) has been thoroughly and permanently blocked by our sin. Try as we might, we can never get right with God by personal righteousness or lawkeeping. But God

---

Scripture Resource: Galatians 3:23—4:7

has not left us to perish. He has graciously provided an alternate route: faith. This is the only genuine road to God and way of salvation for sinners.

In this chapter we want to understand what it means to be "heirs of God's grace." This requires that we first of all understand the difference between these two possible ways of salvation, which may be called *law* and *grace*.

I. The Way of Law

The Bible places the two systems of law and grace in sharp contrast with each other. John says of our Lord, "From the fullness of his grace we have all received one blessing after another. For the law was given through Moses; grace and truth came through Jesus Christ" (John 1:16-17). Paul warns, "You who are trying to be justified by law have been alienated from Christ; you have fallen away from grace" (Galatians 5:4). He says of Christians that we "are not under law, but under grace." (Romans 6:14).

"Under law" is a phrase that describes the state of every person at the beginning of his life. God is a god of "law and order." He created the universe to operate according to natural law, and people to live according to moral law. When a person is born he is already existing within the framework of law. When his moral consciousness develops, a person is confronted with God's moral law, either by general revelation (nature, Romans 1:18-32; 2:14-15) or by special revelation (the Bible).

If a person remains within the system or framework of law, then on the judgment day he will be judged according to the rules or terms of law. (The particular laws under which people live may vary somewhat, but the system of law with its basic ground rules for being saved is the same for everyone.) These rules may be stated very succinctly and simply:

"Keep the law; escape the penalty.
Break the law; suffer the penalty."

This is the way law operates. As long as we are under law, we must realize that these are the rules which apply to us.

This is not so bad, you may say. After all, it *is* possible to be saved under this system. If we keep God's law, we will escape the penalty of hell. If we actually *are* not guilty, then certainly God will have to justify us (declare us "not guilty"). Thus we could be justified by our works, by our obedience to God's commandments.

Yes, it is possible to be justified by works of law—*if* we keep *all* of God's commandments perfectly. The problem is that just one sin makes us a lawbreaker and thus subjects us to the penalty. As James says, "For whoever keeps the whole law, and yet stumbles at just one point, is guilty of breaking all of it" (James 2:10; see Galatians 3:10). Thus to be saved under law (which is where we all begin), one has to live an absolutely sinless life.

Now the terrifying news is that "there is no one righteous, not even one" (Romans 3:10), "for all have sinned and fall short of the glory of God" (Romans 3:23). This means that as long as we remain under law, we are bound to be lost. No amount of subsequent goodness can alter the fact that we have *sinned* and must pay the penalty.

II. The Way of Grace

It is precisely at this point that the gospel is proclaimed: God has provided an alternative to law, another way to be saved. It is the way of *grace.* It is a totally different system, and it operates according to an entirely different set of ground rules. Under grace one approaches God for salvation on these simple terms:

"Keep the law, but suffer the penalty.
Break the law, but escape the penalty."
Hallelujah! Under grace, a lawbreaker (a sinner) may escape the penalty of eternal hell.

"But wait a minute," you say. "Isn't there something wrong with these terms? Why should one who keeps the law suffer the penalty, and one who breaks the law escape the penalty? This doesn't seem fair!''

This is absolutely correct. It is *not* fair. It is not supposed to be. If it were fair, it would not be grace! Law is fair. Grace is more than fair.

"Okay," you say, "but just one more minute. I can accept the second part of the system, i.e., 'Break the law, yet escape the penalty.' That's great, because that's our only hope. But what about that first rule: 'Keep the law, yet suffer the penalty.' Surely this is going too far. How can that be grace? Who would ever agree to that?''

Admittedly, this seems very odd and even objectionable. But remember, grace is different from our ordinary way of thinking. It does not fit within the framework of law and justice and fairness. This is especially true of the statement, "Keep the law, yet suffer the penalty."

But this is the very element of grace that makes it grace! Without this provision, the other one would be impossible. After all, to whom does this provision apply? Who has kept the law, anyway? Only one person: the sinless Christ. Even though He kept the law, He suffered its penalty. Why? For grace! For grace! Only the demands of grace could nail our spotless Lord to the cross. For in His sinless death, He suffered the full penalty of the law *in our place,* and thus made it possible for us as actual lawbreakers to escape the penalty.

The system of grace is summed up perfectly by 2 Corinthians 5:21, "God made him who had no sin to be sin for us, so that in him we might become the righteousness of God.'' Christ took our sins, and we receive His righteousness. God treated Christ like a sinner, so that we can be treated like Him.

Here, then, is the choice with which we are confronted. We can remain under law, to our certain condemnation; or we can accept the free offer of grace and become "heirs of God and co-heirs with Christ" (Romans 8:17). Praise God for this blessed alternative!

III. Heirs of Grace

One thing must be made clear. In distinguishing between law and grace, we are not talking about the difference between the Old Testament and the New Testament. What has been said here about law applies to any form of God's law in any age. The law of Moses is a primary example: no one was ever saved by keeping it. But the same applies to New Testament commandments as well. No one is saved by law-keeping in the New Testament era, even the law recorded in the books of the New Testament. Once a person has sinned, law in any form is helpless to save him.

What, then, was the purpose of the Old Testament law? Paul says it was given "because of transgressions" until Christ should come (Galatians 3:19). This means that it was given to help control man's sinful tendencies, and also to make it clear that everyone *is* a sinner and thus cannot be saved by lawkeeping. Paul says that "through the law we become conscious of sin" (Romans 3:20). Thus the law becomes a schoolmaster or tutor to guide us to Christ as the only source of salvation (Galatians 3:24). The law itself was never intended to be a means of salvation (Galatians 3:21).

This means that Old Testament saints were saved by grace just the same as we are. Abraham is the New Testament's favorite example of this truth. Paul uses Abraham to prove his main point, that "a man is justified by faith apart from observing the law" (Romans 3:28).

The full blessings of salvation and eternal life were offered to Abraham and his family, and through him to all peoples of the earth (Genesis 12:3; Galatians 3:8). How did Abraham receive this glorious inheritance? How did anyone else in the Old Testament era receive it? How does anyone receive it in the New Testament age? Paul says the inheritance does not depend on law, but on God's promise: "God in his grace gave it to Abraham through a promise" (Galatians 3:18). Abraham thus received the blessing through faith in God's promises (see Romans 4:13). "Abraham believed God, and it was credited to him as righteousness" (Genesis 15:6, as quoted in Romans 4:3 and Galatians 3:6).

Paul then makes it clear that this inheritance of grace is shared by everyone in the family of Abraham. Who belongs to Abraham's family? Those who, like Abraham, believe in the promises of God! He is "the father of all who believe" (Romans 4:11).

"You are all sons of God through faith in Christ Jesus, for all of you who were united with Christ in baptism have been clothed with Christ. There is neither Jew nor Greek, slave nor free, male nor female, for you are all one in Christ Jesus. If you belong to Christ, then you are Abraham's seed, and heirs according to the promise" (Galatians 3:26-29).

IV. Living Under Grace

Here is our choice; we can remain under law where our doom is sure, or we can become an heir of God's grace by faith. The decision should not be difficult. If a man is shipwrecked a thousand miles from land and a seaplane lands beside him, he has two options. He can try to swim to shore, or he can get into the plane. Would he hesitate for a moment before getting aboard?

As Christians we have made our decision to live under grace. This is the reasonable and life-giving choice. An important question, however is this: are we actually living in full trust and assurance, taking God at His gracious word? Are we resting our hope of eternal life on the finished work of Christ, trusting in His blood to be the constant covering for our sins? Or are we still living as if we were under law? Are we living as if our salvation actually depends on our daily law-keeping? Are we in fact trusting in our own goodness and works of obedience?

How sad it is to see Christians who still think like the Pharisee in Jesus' parable (Luke 18:9-14). On judgment day, when God asks, "Why should I let you into Heaven?" the Pharisee will say, "Because I have obeyed your commandments." Examine yourself. Is this your attitude? Then you are still thinking in terms of *law,* and you cannot be enjoying the full blessings of God's grace.

The Christian who has grasped the real meaning of grace is like the publican in the same parable. When God asks, "Why should I let you into Heaven?" he will say, "Because I trust in your mercy to forgive my sins." After all, this is His promise, isn't it?

Let us realize that our salvation depends not on our weakness, but on God's strength. It depends not on our ability to keep the law, but on God's ability to keep His promises. When we see this, then we can truly begin to *live* under grace.

Chapter 3

The Right to Freedom

Freedom!
No greater desire burns within the human heart than the desire to be free. There are many kinds of freedom, however. Some are sinful and destructive; some are good and essential.

The best freedom of all is that which comes as a result of the gospel of Jesus Christ. Jesus said, "Then you will know the truth, and the truth will set you free" (John 8:32). Paul adds, "It is for freedom that Christ has set us free. Stand firm, then, and do not let yourselves be burdened again by a yoke of slavery" (Galatians 5:1).

In this chapter we shall seek to understand the meaning of true Christian freedom as it is based upon the gospel truth of justification by faith.

I. False Freedoms

The great emphasis on freedom in our day has caused many to seek to be free in ways that are opposed to

---

Scripture Resource: Galatians 4:8-11; 5:1-10

the gospel. The worst of these is the pursuit of absolute autonomy (i.e., self-rule). This is the desire to be free from all outside authority, including the authority of God. Here a person demands the right to "do his own thing," to set his own standards, to be whatever he feels like being.

A. Absolute Freedom

This is the kind of freedom Satan dangled before Eve when he told her that eating the forbidden fruit would make her like God (Genesis 3:1ff.). This is the kind of freedom *Pepsi-Cola* promotes with its jingle,

There's a feeling around,
It's America's sound,
Pepsi people: feeling free!
Free to choose a new way,
Free to stand up and say:
You be you, and I'll be me!

Many people, especially in the younger generations, have convinced themselves that this is the kind of freedom God intended for us to have. After all, He made us free moral creatures, didn't He? Yes, but this only means that we are free to choose to *do* right or wrong; God alone has the authority to decide what *is* right and wrong. Man is under the illusion of a false freedom when he thinks that he is free to decide for himself what is right and what is wrong.

This freedom is truly false and destructive. It is not really freedom at all. It is slavery to a false idea, the idea that one can really free himself from God's authority. Such pseudo-liberty can lead only to eternal condemnation in hell.

Those who know the gospel of Christ surely would not claim to have this sinful autonomy. Nevertheless, even among Christians, there are some serious misunderstandings about the nature of Christian freedom.

B. Freedom to Disobey

One false concept is the idea that a Christian is free from the obligation to obey God's commands. In its most serious form this has resulted in pure antinomianism. Some have taught that the Christian is obligated to obey no laws at all. They have advocated or permitted all kinds of shameful behavior, all in the name of Christian freedom. After all, if we are justified by *faith,* it doesn't matter what we *do,* does it? This, of course, is a false idea, as Paul shows in Romans 6. (See chapters 7 and 8 of this book).

Most Christians would rightly repudiate such license masquerading as liberty. There is, however, a more subtle kind of license, a semi-autonomy which is practiced by many sincere Christians. This is the idea that we can ignore the *little* obligations and the *lesser* rules as long as we are faithful in the most important things, such as love, mercy, and justice.

Thus such a Christian would never rob his company's payroll, but he thinks nothing of slipping a company screwdriver or box of paper clips into his pocket for home consumption. He would never think of missing the Lord's Supper, but he feels no sense of obligation at all to obey parking laws and speed laws if such are inconvenient. Who are we to worry about such little things, he thinks. Has not Christ set us free from rules? We are not supposed to be *legalists,* are we?

It is true that Jesus condemned the Pharisees who paid all their attention to little things and "neglected the more important matters of the law" (Matthew 23:23). But He shows immediately that it is not an either/or decision; one must be faithful in *both* the small and the large obligations. "You ought to have practiced the latter, without neglecting the former," He said (Matthew 23:23).

The Christian is not free from rules, no matter how small. Stop signs, copyright laws, tax laws—the Christian obeys them *all.* This is not legalism. It is obedience.

23

Legalism is not law-keeping, it is *depending* on law-keeping for being right with God.

Another false idea is that Christian freedom is merely freedom from the Old Testament law with all its jots and tittles. Though this is true to a large extent, our freedom in Christ is much more than this. If one makes this the focal point, he will probably miss the real point of freedom from law.

II. Free From Law

What *does* it mean to be free from law? Here is the key element in Christian freedom, but it must not be misunderstood. As we have stated above, it does *not* mean freedom from obligation to *obey* the law. Nor does it mean simply freedom from the Old Testament form of law. Our liberty is much more glorious than this.

By the word *law* we mean God's moral law in any and all of its forms. If we are free from law, we are free from it even in its New Testament form.

A. Free from Condemnation

We are indeed free from law in several ways. First and most important, we are free from the *condemnation* of the law. Anyone living under law (see chapter 2) must accept the consequences of breaking the law, namely, eternal punishment in hell. Thus every sinner (every one of us) is not only under law, but under its condemnation.

This is the wonderful thing about Jesus Christ: He has borne the condemnation for us. When we put our trust in Him, He frees us from it. "Christ redeemed us from the curse of the law by becoming a curse for us . . ." (Galatians 3:13). This great freedom is expressed in the following hymn:

"Free from the law, O happy condition,
Jesus hath bled, and there is remission;
Cursed by the law and bruised by the fall,
Grace hath redeemed us once for all."

"Now are we free—there's no condemnation,
Jesus provides a perfect salvation;
'Come unto Me,' O hear His sweet call,
Come, and He saves us once for all."

B. Free from Depending on Law-Keeping

Another important aspect of our freedom in Christ is that we are free from the law as a means of justification. As we saw in chapter 2, God has provided an alternative to law: the way of grace. Thus to know that we are justified by faith frees us from thinking that our salvation depends on how well we can obey the law.

The person who thinks his day-by-day obedience is the key to his acceptance with God is a victim either of deception or of despair. If he really thinks he *is* good enough to be accepted by God (like the Pharisee), then he is deceiving himself. Here is the real legalist: the one who depends on his law-keeping to keep him right with God.

On the other hand, the person who thinks he has to be "good enough" for heaven, yet *knows* he is not, will be filled with anxiety, doubt, fear and despair. The meaning of freedom has not yet burst upon him.

The glory of the gospel (justification by faith) is that it frees us both from self-deception and from despair. In Christ we are free from law (i.e., lawkeeping) as a means of being right with God. Romans 10:4 says; "For Christ is the end of the law for righteousness to every one that believeth" (KJV). When we put our trust in Christ, we are confessing that we are *not* able to be good enough for Heaven; but we also cease to worry about it.

C. Free from Legalistic Motives

A final aspect of Christian freedom is that we are free from the law as a taskmaster which forces us to obey—or else! Knowing that we are justified by faith, we can obey the law simply because we *want* to. In other words, the gospel of Christ frees us from legalistic *motives* for obedience.

The Christian life is work. It often takes great effort to live according to God's will. The Bible describes Christian living as taking a yoke, working in a vineyard, reaping a harvest, fighting a battle, bearing a cross, and other such wearisome exercise.

Why does anyone want to work so hard? Why should we persevere in good works? What motivates us?

Living under law, one is driven by the dual motives of fear of punishment and desire for reward. Everything depends on personal obedience. Hence one must obey in order to escape punishment; he must obey in order to gain the reward. He may actually hate the things which God's law requires him to do; but like a sullen slave he does them to escape the whip of God's wrath.

Such motivation is self-centered. It asks, "What's in it for me?" It is like marrying for money. A person so motivated loves salvation rather than the Savior.

The truly Christian motive for good works is grateful love. "If you love me," said Christ, "you will do what I command" (John 14:15). Christian obedience is, as Paul calls it, "labor prompted by love" (1 Thessalonians 1:3). Summing it all up, Galatians 5:6 says that the only thing which matter is "faith which worketh by love" (KJV). In the Christian life a person begins with faith, a faith which works. *Why* does it work? Because of love: the strongest possible motive, the totally self-less motive, the Christ-centered and neighbor-centered motive.

The point is that grace and grace alone frees a person to obey solely from love. Because of grace we are free from punishment on the basis of what *Christ* has done. Jesus paid it *all;* nothing we do adds to His payment. Under grace we are justified by faith, not by works of law (Romans 3:28). Thus if our justification is secure by faith, we are free to work and obey out of selfless and grateful love.

III. Good Works: What Are They?

We experience real freedom when we come to understand the nature of our own works of obedience. They are not a kind of payment which God extorts or demands in return for His saving favors. They are rather our way of saying "Thank you" to a Savior who has freely given us everything.

Martin Luther has summed it up well. He says, "Our faith in Christ does not free us from works but from false opinions concerning works, that is, from the foolish presumption that justification is acquired by works. Faith redeems, corrects, and preserves our consciences so that we know that righteousness does not consist in works, although works neither can nor ought to be wanting. . . ." *(Christian Liberty;* Fortress Press, 1967; pp. 35-36)

Chapter 4

Trademark of Freedom

"For you were called to freedom, brethren; only do not turn your freedom into an opportunity for the flesh, but through love serve one another" (Galatians 5:13 NAS).

The gospel has set us free from law's condemnation and law's compulsion. But Christian freedom is not just freedom *from* something; it is also freedom *for* something. Specifically, we are free to "serve one another in love."

In this chapter we shall see how the gospel sets us free for service to our brethren, and see how this service must be rendered.

I. The Family of Believers

The Bible describes the church as a family or a brotherhood. Galatians 6:10 calls it "the family of believers." We are "members of God's household," says Ephesians 2:19. Peter exhorts us to "love the brotherhood" (1 Peter 2:17). We are children of God (2 Corinthians 6:18)

Scripture Resource: Galatians 5:13-15, 25—6:10

and brothers and sisters to each other (Galatians 5:13; Philemon 2).

Just as certain families have developed coats-of-arms or other unique and distinguishing symbols (e.g., Scottish plaids), so also the family of believers has a distinguishing feature or "trade mark," namely, brotherly love. Jesus said, "A new commandment I give you: Love one another. . . . All men will know that you are my disciples if you love one another" (John 13:34-35).

We are commanded to love all people, even our enemies. But the love we are to have for our fellow Christians is a special kind of love, a *family* love. "Keep on loving each other as brothers," exhorts Hebrews 13:1. (see 1 Peter 3:8.) Romans 12:10 says that we must "be devoted to one another in brotherly love." The term used here is not the ordinary word for Christian love. It is the word which refers to the tender affection found only among family members.

II. Serving in Love

Wherever love exists, it expresses itself in active service. Love cannot be passive. John asks, "If anyone has material possessions and sees his brother in need but has no pity on him, how can the love of God be in him? Dear children, let us not love with words or tongue but with actions and in truth" (1 John 3:17-18). Thus we are to "serve one another in love" (Galatians 5:13). Love for God is shown when we help His people (Hebrews 6:10).

In cases of immediate need we are to help anyone without discrimination (see Luke 10:29-37). But our primary responsibility is to help our fellow Christians. Paul states this clearly: "Therefore, as we have opportunity, let us do good to all people, especially to those who belong to the family of believers" (Galatians 6:10).

A. Spiritual Service

Though we usually fail to see it, our greatest needs are

spiritual. Hence our most important service to our brethren will have to do with spiritual matters.

This is foremost in Paul's mind when he says in Galatians 6:2 that we should "carry each other's burdens." He has just been speaking about helping a brother to overcome a persistent sin (verse 1). When such a one has been restored in repentance, we are then to forgive and comfort him (2 Corinthians 2:7).

The need and responsibility for mutual burden-bearing is seen in the frequent Biblical use of the phrase, "one another" or "each other." Consider this listing:

"Encourage one another daily . . ." (Hebrews 3:13).

"Spur one another on toward love and good deeds" (Hebrews 10:24).

"Encourage one another and build each other up . . ." (1 Thessalonians 5:11).

"Confess your sins to each other and pray for each other . . ." (James 5:16).

"Offer hospitality to one another . . ." (1 Peter 4:9).

"Teach and counsel one another . . ." (Colossians 3:16).

"Have equal concern for each other" (1 Corinthians 12:25).

"Serve one another . . ." (Galatians 5:13).

"As every man hath received the gift, even so minister the same one to another . . ." (1 Peter 4:10, KJV).

This emphasis on mutual service causes us to compare the church to a stone arch, where each unit supports the others. And the overwhelming need in the church is for spiritual support.

B. Works of Benevolence

Love also takes account of the physical needs of the brethren. This is the area of benevolence.

Strangely enough, while most churches have a missions program, very few have a planned program of benevolence. This is strange because the main use of money received in church collections mentioned in the New Testament was for benevolent purposes. The earliest Christians sold property and possessions in order to provide for the daily needs of those who had no means of support (Acts 2:44-45; 4:32-37). When Paul instructed the Corinthian church about their giving (1 Corinthians 16:2; 2 Corinthians 8, 9), he was referring to a collection he was taking for famine-stricken Christians in Jerusalem.

Those who are wealthy (1 Timothy 6:18) and those who have received the spiritual gift of "contributing to the needs of others" (Romans 12:8) have a special responsibility to help others. But, as Paul says, even if it requires hard work, "We must help the weak, remembering the words of the Lord Jesus: 'It is more blessed to give than to receive' " (Acts 20:35). A good example of personal loving service is Dorcas, "who was always doing good and helping the poor" (Acts 9:36-39).

Even in a welfare-state society, there are still many needs and opportunities for churches and individuals to express brotherly love through benevolence. Both in the U.S.A. and abroad, there are a number of Christian children's homes, homes for the elderly, clinics and hospitals which need our support. More often than we realize, individuals in our congregations face special periods of need.

We should remember Paul's teaching in Galatians 6:10, that our primary responsibility is toward the family of believers. As long as there are unmet needs within the church family (even worldwide), these must take precedence over the many pleas that come to us from the secular and denominational world.

III. The Basis of Selfless Service

"Brother Smith and his family have just lost their house and belongings in a fire," the preacher announces. "We are going to pass the collection plate and take a special offering for them." You put a ten-dollar bill into the plate.

"Brother Jones is out of work, and his little girl has been very ill." More bad news. "When the plate is passed, please be as generous as possible." You put in a five-dollar bill.

"Sister Brown hasn't been able to get around very well since she fell last spring. She needs someone to go over to her house and do a bit of cleaning. Is there a volunteer?" You put up your hand.

The deeds are done, and people are helped. Real service has been rendered. But what has been the motivation? In doing good works, are we concerned more with making our own salvation secure than with relieving the needs of others?

A. The *Communio Sanctorum*

To illustrate the difference between these two bases for service, we shall briefly consider the ancient Latin description of the church as a *communio sanctorum* ("communio of the saints").

The medieval Roman Catholic church explained this as meaning "a sharing in the extra merits of the saints." The saints were those few people who were so good and righteous that they had more good works than they needed for their own salvation; thus the excess was added to a "treasury of merits" upon which others could draw.

Martin Luther rightly attacked this interpretation of the *communio sanctorum* for two reasons. First, the only merits which save anyone are those of Jesus. No sinner can gain enough merits to save even himself, much less produce an excess in which others may share.

Second, said Luther, this interpretation makes church membership essentially *selfish.* One becomes a part of the church only for what he can get out of it. If you think salvation can be earned even your own good works are simply benefiting you.

The church *is* a *communio sanctorum,* Luther maintained; but this means simply a "community of the saints." Here the "community" is a community of sharing or living service, and *all* Christians are the "saints." Church membership becomes a means of giving and sharing and expressing love through good works.

What permits us to view church work in this light? Nothing less than justification by faith. We are right with God by faith in *Christ's* merits. Thus we do not have to scurry about, bargaining for someone else's "extra merits" or accumulating a stockpile of our own. Justification by faith replaces self-seeking, meritorious service with selfless, neighbor-centered service. Commenting on Luther's view, Paul Althaus says it well:

"Luther knows that only the gospel of justification by free grace through faith can really create genuine community. Faith in the gospel places man's salvation completely in God's hands and frees man from that selfish concern for his own eternal destiny which had determined all his activity; it thus sets him free to active service of his brethren." *(The Theology of Martin Luther,* p. 303).

"Because the question of our own salvation has been solved in justifying faith, and because a man expects everything from God and nothing from himself, he is now completely free to use all he has, can do, and suffer to serve his brother." *(Ibid.,* p. 308)

B. Rewards for Service

Even though salvation is the free gift of God's grace, and even though our service is motivated by unselfish love, nevertheless our good works will be rewarded by God's own unlimited benevolence. "God . . . will not forget your work and the love you have shown him as you have helped his people and continue to help them" (Hebrews 6:10).

Therefore, "let us not become weary in doing good, for at the proper time we will reap a harvest if we do not give up" (Galatians 6:9).

Chapter 5

Double Trouble

"Whatever happened to sin?" asks the title of a recent book by a well-known psychologist. The answer is that sin is still here, more ugly and prevalent than ever. People just no longer think of it as *sin.*

This is a serious problem, because the gospel of Jesus Christ cannot and will not be understood and accepted until a person is willing to acknowledge the reality and seriousness of sin. The gospel is the answer to man's deepest need. But if the need is not recognized, the gospel will seem superfluous.

In the book of Romans the apostle Paul declares his desire to proclaim the *gospel* to the people in Rome (1:15). The gospel, he says, is God's power for salvation for every believer (1:16). But since Paul at that time could not go to Rome in person, he did the next best thing: he wrote the gospel to them in a letter (the book of Romans).

Following his introductory remarks extolling and emphasizing the gospel ("good news"), Paul begins

---

Scripture Resource: Romans 1:28—2:11

the main body of the letter with some of the harshest and darkest words of condemnation to be found in the Bible: "The wrath of God is being revealed from heaven against all the godlessness and wickedness of men . . ." (1:18). The perverted nature of this wickedness is then detailed in the rest of the chapter (1:18-32).

Does this sound like good news? Certainly not. It is depressing and terrifying. But it is a necessary prelude to the gospel. Sin must be acknowledged before salvation will be accepted. A man must admit he is sick before he will consent to see a doctor.

Here we affirm that fact and the reality of sin. As the apostle says, "There is no one righteous, not even one . . ." (Romans 3:10). Everyone alike is guilty, "for all have sinned and fall short of the glory of God . . ." (Romans 3:23).

Having accepted the *fact* of our sin, we must now turn our primary attention to another question, namely, the *nature* of sin and its consequences. This is also necessary, for how can we appreciate the precise nature of our salvation unless we understand the exact nature of sin?

Our main concern in this chapter, then, is to explain the predicament into which sin has plunged us. We shall see that basically sin has a two-fold effect upon us. It has two principal consequences: it makes us *guilty,* and it makes us *sick.*

I. Sin Makes Us Guilty

The first and primary problem caused by sin is that it makes us guilty. Guilt is not an inward condition; it does not involve our nature or being. It is rather a matter of relationships. To be *guilty* means to be in a wrong relationship with God and with His law. (see 1 John 3:4.)

A. A Legal Problem

As long as we obey God's law, we remain in fellowship with God. When our lives are in harmony with God's law, then we are at peace with God. But when we go against that law, disaster occurs.

Why is "being in trouble with the law" such a serious matter? Because any law involves not only commands to be obeyed, but also penalties to be paid if the law is broken. God's law is no different. It prescribes the penalty of death upon the guilty (Romans 1:32; 6:23). This includes the dreaded second death, which is eternal existence in the fiery lake of hell (Revelation 21:8).

The Bible uses a whole cluster of terms in this connection: judgment, condemnation, damnation, penalty, punishment, wrath. Like the word *guilt,* these are all legal terms and refer to the legal consequences of sin. They are the inevitable, bitter fruit of transgression of the law.

B. The Wrath of God

One item that must be singled out for special emphasis is the wrath of God. Modern man (if he still believes in God at all) tends to deny or explain away the reality of God's wrath. God is loving and kind, it is said; hence He surely cannot experience something so base as wrath or rage.

Such Satanic deception is directly opposed by the Word of God. Nothing is more dreadfully real than the wrath of the Lord. Nahum the prophet asks, "Who can stand before his indignation? and who can abide in the fierceness of his anger? his fury is poured out like fire, and the rocks are thrown down by him" (Nahum 1:6, KJV). Another prophet warned, "Gather yourselves together . . . before the fierce anger of the LORD come upon you, before the day of the LORD'S anger come upon you" (Zephaniah 2:1-2, KJV). Even Jesus exhibited wrath (Mark 3:5) and warned of hell (Matthew 10:28). Men shall flee in terror from the "wrath of the Lamb" when "the great day of their wrath" comes (Revelation 6:16-17).

God is not fickle nor His wrath unpredictable. We know exactly what arouses His anger; it is directed against "godlessness and wickedness" (Romans 1:18). Sin draws the wrath of God like a magnet draws iron. "Our God is a consuming fire" (Hebrews 12:29).

One consequence of sin, then, is that it makes us guilty. We stand condemned by the law and threatened by God's wrath.

II. Sin Makes Us Sick

A second main effect of sin is that it makes us sick. We are not speaking of physical illness, though this may happen occasionally. We are referring rather to a sickness of the soul. When we sin, our spiritual nature becomes weakened and corrupted.

In other words, sin affects not just our *relationship* to God and His law; it also affects us personally. Our very nature, our very condition is affected. We become sinful; we are spiritually diseased.

A. A Sinful Nature

There are some who say that only actions can be sinful; people themselves are not sinful. This is erroneous. People are not only *sinners* (i.e., persons who sin), but also are *sinful*. Sinfulness infects the soul like a disease. "One of the most difficult lessons for us to learn," someone has said, "is that sin is not only what we *do*, but also what we are. Sin, in the form of corruption, is in our very nature."

On the other hand, there are many who say that every person is *totally* corrupt and is even *born* that way. This, too, is erroneous. Our natures are depraved, but not completely so; and they are depraved as a result of our own sins (see Ephesians 2:1—we are dead in our *own* trespasses and sins).

The Bible's teaching is clear. For example, Jesus compares a person and his actions to a tree and its fruit. In saying that a corrupt tree produces bad fruit, He shows that evil resides in our very natures. "A bad tree bears bad fruit," He says (Matthew 7:17). He uses this simile again in Matthew 12:33-35, concluding that "the evil man brings evil things out of the evil stored up in him."

The Bible often describes man's spiritual condition in terms of physical and mental ailments. Isaiah gives this graphic picture: "The whole head is sick, and the whole heart faint. From the sole of the foot even unto the head there is no soundness in it; but wounds, and bruises, and putrifying sores: they have not been closed, neither bound up, neither mollified with ointment" (Isaiah 1:5-6, KJV).

The sinful condition is one of weakness (Romans 5:6). We are spiritually blind (Romans 3:18; Revelation 3:17). Our mouth, tongue, and lips are diseased (Romans 3:13-14). We are feeble-minded (Romans 3:11; 8:7; 2 Timothy 3:8;). The heart, which in Scripture represents man's inner spiritual nature, is weak and diseased (Jeremiah 16:12; Ezekiel 36:26; Ephesians 4:18; Matthew 15:19). As Jeremiah says, "The heart is deceitful above all things, and desperately wicked" (Jeremiah 17:9, KJV).

Our spiritual condition is so bad that it is called a state of *death.* We are spiritually dead (Ephesians 2:1, 5; Colossians 2:13). As Alexander Campbell sums up this state of sinfulness, "Without faith every man is spiritually blind, and dead to the things of God, of Christ, and heaven" *(Christian Baptism,* p. 231).

B. Sins and Sinfulness

It is easy to see that we *do* things that are evil, but it is difficult to acknowledge that we ourselves are sinful. We would rather think of ourselves as normal or neutral, like a white sheet of paper. Our sins would then be like black spots on the white paper.

What we need to see is that the paper *itself* is black, so that naturally every portion of it is black. When the heart is corrupt, naturally it will give rise to sinful acts.

We wonder why there is so much evil in the world. We wonder why people commit so many sins. Why cannot everyone just begin to do good? What causes the sins?

Once a person has yielded to temptation and committed that first sin, he becomes the victim of a vicious cycle. The more he sins, the more sinful he becomes; and the more sinful he becomes, the more he sins.

It is because we have developed a sinful nature and *are* evil that we do evil things. We commit sins because we have a corrupt heart. Again, Jesus appeals to the tree and its fruit to illustrate this point. "Likewise," He says, "every good tree bears good fruit, but a bad tree bears bad fruit" (Matthew 7:17).

Another time He says, "Make a tree good and its fruit will be good, or make a tree bad and its fruit will be bad, for a tree is recognized by its fruit. You brood of vipers, how can you who are evil say anything good? For out of the overflow of the heart the mouth speaks. The good man brings good things out of the good stored up in him, and the evil man brings evil things out of the evil stored up in him" (Matthew 12:33-35).

The problem, says Jesus, is the evil heart. "But the things that come out of the mouth come from the heart, and these make a man 'unclean.' For out of the heart come evil thoughts, murder, adultery, sexual immorality, theft, false testimony, slander" (Matthew 15:18-19).

Visible, discernible sins are no more than symptoms of a dreadful inner disease. Like red spots or a fever or a hacking cough, they signal the presence of something worse within.

What, then, is a person to do when he finds himself to be continually telling lies, saying evil words, thinking lustful thoughts, and cheating his neighbors? Can he just quit doing these things, thus reforming his life? No, this will not solve his problem. Overcoming a sinful practice apart from salvation through Jesus Christ is like suppressing a symptom but allowing the disease to rage on un-checked within. It will surely break out again.

The only solution to the problem of sins is to cure the sinfulness. We must be rid of the disease itself, not just the symptoms.

III. Double Trouble

Sin has thus left us with a kind of "double trouble." First, we are guilty and thus are condemned by God's law. Second, we are spiritually corrupted and thus more likely to sin.

The twofold nature of the problem can be illustrated in this way. Imagine a short-tempered husband who (un-justly, of course) becomes angry with his wife. He stalks out of the house, gets into his car, and roars off down the street. At the intersection he ignores the stop sign, zooms out onto the highway, and promptly collides with a truck.

As a result of his escapade, this man has double trouble. He has a legal problem, since he ran through a stop sign and caused an accident. Consequently he must face policemen, lawyers, judges, and a large fine. On the other hand, he has developed a medical problem, since he broke his leg in the accident. This is a very different kind of problem, and will be treated in a different way (emergency room, doctors, cast).

The bad news for the sinner is that he, too, has a legal problem and a health problem because of sin. The good news, however, is that both can be overcome by the grace and power of Jesus Christ. For the double trouble, there is a double cure. The next two chapters will discuss the aspects of the cure.

Chapter 6

No Easy Way

The answer to the problem of our guilt is justification, or forgiveness.

Some may think it is an easy thing for God to forgive a sinner. A popular song once said, "Though it makes Him sad to see the way we live, He'll always say, 'I forgive.' "

But is it such a simple matter? Does God merely need to nod His head in our direction and say, "I forgive you"? To be forgiven or justified, we may recall, means to be declared "not guilty." How can God look us directly in the face and pronounce us not guilty, when He *knows* we *are* guilty?

There is only one answer to this question. We are, as Paul says, "justified by his blood" (Romans 5:9). But how does the death of Christ provide a basis for forgiveness? And why is it the *only* way we can be justified?

In this chapter we will seek the meaning of Christ's death as a *propitiation*. This will explain how we can, through Jesus Christ, be reconciled to God.

Scripture Resource: Romans 5:1-11

I. Propitiation

Why did Jesus die on the cross? So that God might be both *just,* and the *justifier* of those who believe in Jesus (Romans 3:26). Here is the answer in a nutshell.

Ordinarily we think of the cross as being necessary for our sakes, but this is true only in a secondary sense. Certainly our salvation depends on the cross; as sinners we can be saved in no other way. Yet, in the final analysis, the cross is necessary not just because we are sinners, but because God is God. The necessity of the cross is rooted in the nature of God!

Romans 3:26 says that Jesus died so that God might be perfect in two ways: as just and as justifier. We see that God is not arbitrarily choosing one thing rather than another. He is expressing His very nature. The nature of God requires that He be both just and justifier, because His nature embraces both justice and love.

How do these two attributes of God make the cross necessary?

A. God Is Just

Someone may ask, "If God is all-powerful, why can't He just forgive sins apart from the cross? Why doesn't He just say, 'I forgive you'? Why doesn't He just brush away our sins and save us by His sovereign decree? The answer lies in the justice of God.

"For all his ways are justice: a God of faithfulness and without iniquity, just and right is he" (Deuteronomy 32:4, ASV).

Justice or righteousness is that characteristic of God which requires Him to punish sin. Sin is the transgression of God's law, and the law is the expression of God's own nature. Sin therefore is the transgression of the nature of God, a virutal attempt to contradict God.

For example, the command not to lie springs from the very nature of God, who is truth. God cannot lie (Titus 1:2); therefore it is a violation of His character for creatures made in His image to lie. When we tell a lie, then, we are not just breaking some abstract law which God has arbitrarily made; we are in fact assaulting God himself.

When God's nature thus has been attacked and contradicted, by a lie or by any other sin, what must God do? Can God overlook that which blasphemes His very character? Certainly not. God cannot shut His eyes and pretend that lies and murders and adulteries do not exist. His justice will not permit it. This is why the law carries a penalty for sin. God is just; and when His own nature is violated, that violation must be punished, or God is not true to himself.

Here, then, is the necessity. God must punish sin because He is a just God. His justice cannot treat sin lightly. His justice kindles the flame of His wrath, which utterly consumes sin. The fury of His justice must be poured out on every sinner. "Our God is a consuming fire" (Hebrews 12:29).

B. God Is Love

At this point someone objects again. "You say that God is God, and God is just. Very well, then. Let God be God! Let Him be just and punish our sin. Let Him cast us all into hell this very moment. Let Him inflict the penalty which His eternal law demands." As a matter of fact, justice would be satisfied if every sinner were punished eternally in hell. God's justice could be satisfied without the cross.

Then why does God not do this? Why does He not give us all what we deserve instead of sending Jesus to the cross? Because God is also *love!* (see 1 John 4:8.) If justice were all that needed to be satisfied, then God could send us to hell and be perfectly true to His nature. But God is also love, and loves does not desire that any should perish (2 Peter 3:9; 1 Timothy 2:4). Therefore if all men perish, then God would not be true to His nature as love. This is why God must be not only just, but justifier as well. That is, He must pronounce us righteous so that His wrath does not consume us.

From our standpoint the nature of God presents a dilemma, an impossible requirement. Love is the nature of God, and love desires our salvation. But justice is also the nature of God, and justice requires our damnation.

Mortals have no answer to this "problem fit for God." Its solution, however, is not beyond the all-wise Savior. The answer to our humanly-conceived dilemma is part of His eternal plan. That answer is the death of His only begotten Son on the cross.

The justice and love of God require Him both to punish sin and to save the sinner. It is this apparently impossible task which makes the cross necessary. In the cross God is both just and justifier.

C. He Died for Us

How does the cross meet this dilemma arising from the nature of God? What is there about the cross which makes it the answer to the problem? Basically, because it is a propitiation.

A propitiation is an offering that turns away wrath. For instance, let us imagine that the ill-tempered husband who treated his wife unjustly (see chapter 5) repents and desires to make amends. Thus he visits the florist and returns home with a dozen roses. The flowers are a propitiation—an offering designed to turn his wife's wrath away from him.

The Bible describes Christ's death as a propitiation (Romans 3:25; 1 John 2:2; 4:10, KJV). This means that Jesus satisfied God's righteous, judicial demand for justice by accepting upon himself all the wrath and punishment which sin justly deserves.

Christ died "for our sins" (1 Corinthians 15:3). Christ "himself bore our sins in his body on the cross" (1 Peter 2:24). What does it mean to say that he "bore our sins"? This concept is brought more clearly into focus by two other striking expressions: Christ was "made . . . to be sin for us" (2 Corinthians 5:21), and he became "a curse for us" (Galatians 3:13).

Though He was not personally guilty of sin, Jesus was brought into so close an identification with sin that He could in His own person bear the curse due to sin. When we say that Christ "bore our sins," we mean more specifically that He bore the *penalty* for them; He bore the full force of the wrath of God against our sins. In thus allowing the penalty of sin to be inflicted on himself, Christ satisfied God's justice and became our propitiation.

That Christ suffered the penalty for sin enables God to be just; that He suffered it *for us* enables God to be justifier. We cannot ignore the emphasis on substitution in the passages quoted above. It was "for us" that He died. He satisfied God's wrath in our place, as our substitute.

Because the cross is what it is, God can forgive our sins and justify us, and be just at the same time. If Christ suffered the penalty for our sins, then our sins have already been punished in Him. The fiery wrath of God due to us has already burned itself out on Him. Therefore when God says to us, "You are forgiven," He is not simply brushing our sins aside. On the contrary, every sin which is forgiven in us has already been punished in Christ. Because of Christ, God can be both just and justifier.

II. Justification

Because Christ is our propitiation, we can be "justified by his blood" (Romans 5:9), "through faith in his blood" (Romans 3:25). God will justify even the wicked (Romans 4:5), if the wicked will put their trust in Christ's atoning death.

Guilty? Yes, but through faith the blood of Christ covers the sin and absorbs the guilt. Thus God can treat the sinner just as if he were *not* guilty. To say that I am *justified* means that God treats me *"just as if I'd"* never sinned.

45

Sinners? Yes, but God does not hold our sins against us if we are under the blood of Christ. He does not condemn us. "Therefore, there is now no condemnation for those who are in Christ Jesus" (Romans 8:1).

III. Reconciliation

Those who are justified through faith in Jesus' blood live in a state of peace with God. "Therefore," Paul says, "since we have been justified through faith, we have peace with God through our Lord Jesus Christ" (Romans 5:1).

The accomplishment of peace between God and man is another aspect of the atoning work of Christ. It takes into consideration the fact that as sinners, we were God's enemies. There was enmity and hatred between us and God. But here again the love of God is shown, because even "when we were God's enemies, we were reconciled to him through the death of his Son" (Romans 5:10).

There are two steps to our reconciliation to God. First, God's enmity toward us must be removed. Some find it difficult to accept the Biblical teaching that a God of love could ever have enmity toward His creatures. Isaiah teaches, however, that our sins cause God to turn His face away from us (Isaiah 59:2). He cannot behold evil nor look upon iniquity (Habakkuk 1:13). Sinners are the objects of divine hatred (Proverbs 6:19).

It is God's enmity toward us that is removed by the propitiating death of Christ. Even while *we* were *still* God's enemies, Christ's death reconciled us (Romans 5:10). The reconciliation was something He accomplished before we even knew about it, before it was even proclaimed to us. By diverting His wrath and enmity wholly upon Jesus, God cleared away every obstacle to reconciliation and peace from His side.

The second step toward reconciliation is our own acceptance of what God has done for us. When the "message of reconciliation" is proclaimed to us, we must put away *our* enmity and "be reconciled to God" (2 Corinthians 5:19-20). In this way we receive the already-accomplished reconciliation as our very own (Romans 5:11). Once again we are friends of God, living in peace with Him.

Yes, God has solved the problem of our guilt, but not without great cost to himself. It required the death of His only-begotten Son, upon whom, as our substitute, the divine wrath and enmity were poured out.

Chapter 7

Double Cure

As we have seen, sin produces a kind of "double trouble": guilt and spiritual sickness. We have seen how God solves the problem of our guilt in a wonderful way. But what of the sickness? What of the sinfulness in our souls?

Christ solves this problem, too. What else should we expect from a Savior who "is able to save completely" (Hebrews 7:25)? If there is "double trouble," he can provide a "double cure"!

> Rock of Ages, cleft for me;
> Let me hide myself in thee.
> Let the water and the blood
> From thy wounded side which flowed
> Be of sin the double cure:
> Save me from its guilt and power.

Our God not only saves us from the consequences of guilt; He also gives us the strength necessary to over-

---

Scripture Resource: Romans 6:12-23

come sin's power. He not only saves us from wrath; He makes us pure. He gives us new life and new spiritual power from within, thus enabling us to defeat Satan and overcome temptation. This process of recovery from sin-sickness begins with regeneration or the new birth; its continuation is referred to as sanctification.

Other familiar hymns refer meaningfully to this "double cure." We sing of the "old rugged cross" on which Jesus suffered and died "to *pardon* and *sanctify* me." We have "blessed assurance" that we are "born of his Spirit, washed in his blood." (To be washed or cleansed means to be forgiven; the guilt is removed.) The Savior who, like a Shepherd leads us, also gives us "grace to cleanse and power to free." Thus is "sin pardoned, man restored" *(Thy Hand, O God, Has Guided).*

The concept of the double cure is firmly grounded in Scripture. The dual nature of salvation is prophesied in Ezekiel 36:25-27. Verse 25 refers to the cleansing from guilt: "Then will I sprinkle clean water upon you, and ye shall be clean" (KJV). The next two verses then describe the new birth through the Holy Spirit: "A new heart also will I give you, and a new spirit will I put within you: and I will take away the stony heart out of your flesh, and I will give you an heart of flesh. And I will put my Spirit within you, and cause you to walk in my statutes, and ye shall keep my judgments, and do them" (KJV).

Jesus sums it up in His instruction to Nicodemus: "I tell you the truth, unless a man is born of *water* and the *Spirit,* he cannot enter the kingdom of God" (John 3:5). Peter reflects the double cure in his two-fold promise on the day of Pentecost: "Repent and be baptized, every one of you, in the name of Jesus Christ so that your sins may be forgiven. And you will receive the gift of the Holy Spirit" (Acts 2:38).

In this chapter our goal will be to learn more about how God cures our sinfulness by giving us new life in Christ.

I. What Is the New Life?

The concept of justification by faith, rightly understood, is radically extraordinary. It is so different from anything our sin-conditioned minds would expect, that many cannot bring themselves to believe it.

On the other hand, its radical nature leads some to an entirely false and unwarranted conclusion. If we are justified by faith, they say, then our works are irrelevant, and we can sin as much as we want.

What shall we say, then? Is justification by faith a license to sin? By no means! This, of course, is the objection which Paul anticipated in Romans 6. His answer to this false reasoning is simple. Those who conclude this, he says, have a too-limited understanding of salvation. They do not see that salvation is more than just forgiveness (justification). Salvation also involves receiving a *new life,* a life where righteousness is the rule and sin the exception.

"We died to sin," Paul says; "how can we live in it any longer?" (Romans 6:2). It is a moral contradiction, contrary to all reason. The old self, the heart that was inclined to sin and enjoyed sinning, was put to death—crucified with Christ. Thus we have been released from the enslaving power of sin (Romans 6:6-7).

This death of the old sinful nature is accompanied by the gift of a *new* nature, a *new* heart, a *new* life. Jesus died yet rose again; "In the same way, count yourselves dead to sin but alive to God in Christ Jesus" (Romans 6:11). Remember Ezekiel's prophecy: "A new heart also will I give you, and a new spirit will I put within you" (Ezekiel 36:26, KJV).

This change in our inner nature is described in many different ways in the New Testament. Each of the expressions used emphasizes the radical character of the change. Here is a listing:

a) *Resurrection.* Paul brings out this concept in Romans 6, but it appears in many other places as well. (See

Ephesians 2:6; Colossians 2:12; 3:1.) At conversion, the soul which was "dead in transgressions and sins" (Ephesians 2:1) is literally raised from the dead. It is the spiritual counterpart and fore-runner of the resurrection of the body at the return of Jesus.

b) *Quickening.* This is an old word which has all but passed out of usage since the days of the *King James Version.* It means simply "making alive," and is so translated in most modern versions. It is obviously a synonym for *resurrection* and is used in exactly the same way. When we became Christians, God "made us alive with Christ" (Ephesians 2:5). See also John 5:21, 25; 1 John 3:14; Colossians 2:13. These two expressions taken together form the most common and most significant way of describing the change in our natures.

c) *Regeneration.* Mistranslated "rebirth" in the *New International Version* (Titus 3:5), this term literally means a "beginning-again," or a new beginning. This emphasizes the gracious opportunity given with the new life.

d) *Renewal.* Here again the idea of newness is foremost. (See Titus 3:5; Ephesians 4:23.)

e) *New Creation.* Nothing indicates the radical nature of the new life more than this term. "Therefore, if anyone is in Christ, he is a new creation; the old has gone, the new has come!" (2 Corinthians 5:17; see also Galatians 6:15; Ephesians 2:10).

f) *Rebirth.* The root word used for this concept can mean either "begotten" or "born." The distinction here is not significant; either way it refers to the turning-point from death or no-life to a new and living existence. (The equivalence between birth and resurrection can be seen in the expression, "firstborn from the dead," Revelation 1:5; see Colossians 1:18.) Although the expression "born again" enjoys wide use among Christian people, it does not occur in the Bible nearly as often as the expressions "resurrection" and "made alive." See John 3:3-5; 1 Peter 1:3, 22-23.

g) *Circumcision.* This last term emphasizes the negative aspect of the death or removal of the old sinful nature. It refers to a spiritual operation upon the heart or soul and as such is parallel to the terms already listed. It is a common expression: see Colossians 2:11-13; Acts 7:51; Romans 2:29; Philippians 3:3.

All of these expressions are just different ways of referring to a radical change within us, the result of which is a new nature, a new heart, a new life.

II. When Is the New Life Received?

When we examine the dynamic expressions listed above, we are overwhelmed at what God has promised to do for us. Perhaps some of us are wondering, "Did all this really happen to *me?* If so, *when?"* Others may be saying, "I *want* this to happen to me! When can I receive it?"

The answer is clearly stated in the New Testament: the change occurs during Christian baptism. Paul says, "Or don't you know that all of us who were baptized into Christ Jesus were baptized into his death? We were therefore buried with him through baptism into death in order that, just as Christ was raised from the dead through the glory of the Father, we too may live a new life" (Romans 6:3-4). This has to refer to the Christian's water-baptism. Those who try to separate water-baptism from the inner baptism of the Holy Spirit go against Scripture (Ephesians 4:4—there is only *one* baptism).

The clearest statement of all is Colossians 2:12, which says specifically that "in baptism you were buried with him and raised with him." Of course, this happens only "through your faith in the power of God." (See also John 3:5; Titus 3:5; Acts 2:38.)

How do we know that it happens at baptism and not at some other point in time? Simply because this is the clear teaching and promise of God. We must not expect some warm inner feeling or emotional experience necessarily to strike us in order to validate the promise. God keeps His promises when we accept them in faith.

A great host of Bible-believing people sincerely believe that God gives the new birth prior to baptism, namely, as soon as one believes. Please get this point absolutely clear: the Bible says that our forgiveness and renewal are given *through* faith, but this does not mean "*as soon as* one believes." In fact, the teaching is clearly otherwise. It happens *through* faith, but *in* baptism (Colossians 2:12).

Some will admit that baptism is the point of the new *birth,* but they extend the metaphor to imply that a conception or begetting had to occur *prior* to the birth. Hence, it is said, the new life has already begun prior to baptism.

This extension of the metaphor is unjustified, however; and it is absolutely ruled out when we realize that the metaphor of birth is just one among many which describe the new beginning. Equivalent to it, and much more prominent to Scripture, is the concept of resurrection. When we see the significance of all these terms together, particularly *resurrection* and *quickening,* we will see that the notion of a change in two stages (conception and birth) contradicts the very point they are making.

One other point should be noted here. Some have thought that the change in our nature is something which we ourselves accomplish via repentance. When we repent, we resolve to forsake sin and live a life of righteousness; we determine to be a different person and to change our lives completely. This change of mind and heart is said to be the new birth.

This cannot be, however. The one thing that should strike us when we examine the list of expressions describing this change is that it is something so enormously radical that it could never be accomplished merely by our puny self-resolve. It is a *resurrection.* It is an act of *creation.* It is a *regeneration.* Such a change cannot be wrought by human power (see Colossians 2:11). It is not something we *do;* it is something *done to* us.

The one who works this work upon our hearts is the Holy Spirit, who is given to us in baptism (Acts 2:38) for this very purpose. We are "born of water and the Spirit" (John 3:5). Our baptism is "the washing of rebirth and renewal by the Holy Spirit" (Titus 3:5). This is God's promise. Let this be our faith.

III. The Purpose of the New Life

God gives us the gift of new life in Christ to enable us to live righteously before Him.

While living in unbelief we were slaves to sin (Romans 6:17-21). Because of the weakness of our sinful natures, we readily yielded to temptation. Sin (as someone has said), though not necessary, was inevitable.

But a change occurs when we receive the new life. The power of sin is broken, and we are able to resist temptation and obey God's commandments.

Thus, because you are dead to sin and alive to God in Jesus Christ, "do not let sin reign in your mortal body" (Romans 6:12). Rather, "offer yourselves to God, as those who have returned from death to life" (Romans 6:13).

Of course, we begin this life as babies and thus will not live it in perfection at first. But the purpose and responsibility of the Christian is to *grow* in his new life, to become more and more holy and spiritual (Matthew 5:48; 1 Peter 1:16). This process is called sanctification (1 Thessalonians 5:23). Thank God for its possibilities!

Chapter 8

Only the Beginning

The beginning of new life described in the preceding chapter is probably the most significant change that any of us will experience. Yet, we must remember that it is only the *beginning* of new life. It opens the way to profound possibilities for further change. We are now free to develop all our potential as creatures made in the very image of God.

The reality of rebirth is an inner change of the heart, a change in our basic nature. It is something that we cannot be directly conscious of; we accept it by faith. The important thing is that this makes it possible for us to alter all the areas of our lives of which we *are* conscious. Our habits, our actions, our speech, our thoughts, our preferences, our desires, even our motives—all of these are free from slavery to sin and free to be conformed to the pattern of God's holiness.

This, in fact, must be the Christian's primary task. We can and we must change. We must grow. It will not hap-

Scripture Resource: Romans 7:14—8:2

pen automatically, however. We must make the decision, and we must do it, using the enabling power and freedom provided by the Holy Spirit.

I. The Need to Change

Change is necessary as long as there is imperfection. The only things that ought to stay the same are the things that are perfect.

When we study God's Word and gain more knowledge of His holiness and His law, one thing is made perfectly clear to us. We learn what a long way we are from perfection! As Romans 3:20 says, "Through the law we become conscious of sin."

In Romans 7:7-13 Paul describes his own deepening consciousness of sin through his knowledge of God's law. For instance, if he had not become aware of the commandment, "Do not covet," he would never have known what covetousness was or that he was coveting.

Wouldn't it be better not to know the commandments, then? No, indeed, for then one would be following the way of death and not even be aware of it. Knowledge of the law makes one aware of his sin and his spiritual death. Such knowledge is necessary "in order that sin might be recognized as sin, . . . so that through the commandment sin might become utterly sinful" (7:13).

Even after we have been born again through the Holy Spirit at baptism, we must continue to use God's law as a searchlight for our lives, to show us where we need to change. We are now alive, and a living organism must change and grow or it will die.

A. Growth in Knowledge

We must grow in our *knowledge.* This comes only from studying the Bible. By studying the Old Testament we come to know how God prepared a people, the Jews, to receive the world's Savior when He became a human being. By studying the gospels we learn of the Savior's life, teachings, death and resurrection. By studying the book of Acts we come to know how the church, the kingdom of Christ, began and grew. By studying the rest of the New Testament we learn how the Savior wants His church and His people to live until He returns.

Through such study, and through participation in the life of the church, we not only learn facts, but also come to know Jesus Christ himself more intimately.

In Hebrews 5:11—6:3, God rebukes us all for neglecting to grow in knowledge. Many of us are no further than the baby bottle, he says, when we ought to be eating the solid food of the deeper teachings of the Bible. Everyone should study as if he were preparing to be a teacher of the Word (5:12). "And God permitting, we will do so" (6:3).

B. Growth in Attitudes

The second area of growth is in our *attitudes,* our whole inner life, our mental and spiritual states. Our desires and preferences must change. Sinful and self-centered attitudes must be replaced by unselfish and God-honoring desires. Hate and indifference must be replaced by love. We must cease to be motivated by fear and greed, and let love motivate us instead. We must bring our temperament under control, letting God fill us with a spirit of sweetness and kindness.

Jesus tells us the kinds of attitudes He wants in the "beatitudes" of Matthew 5:1-10. He says that we must develop meekness, humility, mercy, purity of heart, and other such graces. Paul gives a similar listing in Galatians 5:22-23. He names love, joy, peace, patience, kindness, goodness, faithfulness, gentleness, and self-control. (see also 2 Peter 1:5-6; Philippians 4:8.)

Probably the most difficult changes we will have to make are in this area of attitudes. It will take time. The process may be painful and slow. But it is most important, and we must diligently work at it.

C. Growth in Good Works

Finally, we must also grow in our good works, in our outward behavior or manner of life. We must conquer sinful habits and avoid sinful activities. We must develop a Christ-honoring pattern of spiritual habits and exercises. We must live a life of love, obedience, and good works.

II. The Desire to Change

Children are usually impatient to grow up. Little girls put on Mommie's dress and shoes and make-up. Young boys are eager to be old enough to drive a car. They all desire to reach the age of maturity.

This must also be the deep desire of the Christian from the time he is born again. "Like newborn babies, crave pure spiritual milk, so that by it you may grow up in your salvation" (1 Peter 2:2). We must really want to change from the weakness and frustrations of infancy to the strength and joy of accomplishment that come with maturity.

We do not expect a new-born infant to get up and run the 100-yard dash. Nor do we expect the new Christian to begin immediately to live a perfect, mature life. At our own various stages of growth, we all know that we are not what we ought to be. We are still plagued by unwanted sin. This does not mean that we are lost, of course. Even though we are imperfect sinners, we are justified through Christ. "Therefore, there is now no condemnation for those who are in Christ Jesus" (Romans 8:1).

What is of utmost importance for growing Christians is the *sincere desire* to change. We may often find ourselves frustrated by nagging sin, as Paul did: "For I have the desire to do what is good, but I cannot carry it out. For what I do is not the good I want to do; no, the evil I do not want to do—this I keep on doing" (Romans 7:18-19).

What made Paul different from an unbelieving sinner?

Not his lack of sin, but his *desire* not to sin. He *wanted* to quit sinning and to be good.

Even with the desire to overcome sin, will we be able to do it? Must we continue to be frustrated in our efforts to mature in Christian attitudes and behavior? The answer is summed up in an old proverb: "Where there is a will, there is a way." When our will is truly committed to the desire to change, a way of freedom and power to change is at our disposal.

III. The Freedom to Change

The freedom to change is the gracious gift of God. It is nothing less than the "gift of the Holy Spirit" (Acts 2:38). The Holy Spirit himself is given to us to dwell in us, in our very lives and bodies (1 Corinthians 6:19). His liberating presence frees us from the power of sin and helps us to return to a state of spiritual health and purity.

A. The Presence of the Holy Spirit

A non-Christian does not have the spiritual resources to live a godly life. He is powerless (Romans 5:6) to overcome sin on his own. Paul makes this very clear in Romans 8:5-8. "Those who live according to their sinful nature have their minds set on what that nature desires. . . . The mind of sinful man is death . . . because the sinful mind is hostile to God. It does not submit to God's law, nor can it do so. Those controlled by their sinful nature cannot please God."

The sinner is like a person controlled by an impairing disease. He cannot make his feet go where they should. He cannot make his hands do what they should. He cannot make his mouth say what it should. But—he *can* surrender himself to a doctor, who can give him treatment and medicine that will bring his body back under his own control again.

Likewise the sinner can yield himself to the Great Physician, who fills his life and body with the Holy Spirit himself. Through His healing and liberating presence, the power of sin is broken. As Paul says, "You, however, are controlled not by your sinful nature but by the Spirit, if the Spirit of God lives in you" (Romans 8:9; see verse 11).

If the Spirit of God *lives in you!* Yes, this is precisely what happens to those who become Christians. The very Holy Spirit of God comes to take residence in our very bodies (1 Corinthians 6:19). This is one of the blessings of the New Covenant age. Ezekiel prophesied it (36:27), and Jesus promised it (John 7:37-39). On the Day of Pentecost it was announced that the Spirit would be given to those who meet the Giver in Christian baptism (Acts 2:38).

How do we know the Holy Spirit lives in us? Because God has made a promise. He promised to give us the Spirit in baptism. If we have met Him there in full surrender, then the Spirit is present in us. We need no more assurance than God's promise. To require more is to doubt God's Word.

The Christian, then, *does* have the spiritual resources to live a godly life, namely, the presence of the Holy Spirit. The Spirit enables us to do what we could not do by ourselves. He gives us victory over our own sinful nature.

B. The Power of the Holy Spirit

Many people have misunderstood the purpose of the Spirit's presence in us. They have thought that the Holy Spirit is in us in order to give us some kind of *knowledge.* After all, the Bible does speak of being "led by the Spirit of God" (Romans 8:14). Thus many have come to expect some kind of inner knowledge or guidance from the Spirit.

This is not why the Spirit is given to us, however. The Spirit has already given us *knowledge* through the inspired Word of God (see 2 Peter 1:21). Our problem is not that we do not *know* what to do. Our problem is not being

60

able to live according to what we already know. This is why we need the Spirit.

The purpose of the Spirit's presence in us can be summed up in one word: power. The Spirit is the source of the spiritual energy and moral power we need to be able to obey God's law. It is "by the Spirit" that we "put to death the misdeeds of the body" (Romans 8:13). This is what it means to be "led by the Spirit": we let Him show us the way in the Bible, and we let Him reinforce our will and determination to walk in that way.

Here is the meaning of Philippians 2:13, which says that "it is God who works in you to will and to work for his good pleasure" (RSV). Paul also prays "that out of his glorious riches he may strengthen you with power through his Spirit in your inner being" (Ephesians 3:16). The Spirit gives us power to resist temptation (see 1 Corinthians 10:13) and to grow in holiness.

Many sincere Christians *want* to change their lives but are often unsuccessful because they rely on their own strength and will power. This is not enough, nor is it all that is available. Let us begin to take full advantage of the Spirit's power within us.

When faced with temptation, we must pause and pray, consciously trusting the Holy Spirit to supply us with determination to resist. We must also pray specifically for the Spirit to help us develop the attitudes we want and ought to have as Christians. Of course, our will must be fully yielded to the Spirit, because He will not aid us against our will. To the heart fully surrendered, however, He gives freedom and power.

Chapter 9

How Can I Be Sure?

"Blessed assurance, Jesus is mine! Oh, what a foretaste of glory divine!"

"When the roll is called up yonder, *I'll be there."*

"Yes, *my name's written there,* on the page white and fair, in the book of God's kingdom—yes, my name's written there!"

"Onward to the prize before us! Soon his beauty we'll behold, Soon the pearly gates will open; *we shall* tread the streets of gold."

Many of our favorite hymns express the confident expectation of eternal life. We sing them Sunday after Sunday. But do we really mean it? Do we really consider ourselves "ready for the judgment day"?

The Bible definitely teaches that we may have assurance. We may know ourselves to be secure in God's love. This is the very meaning of the Biblical word hope. In the Bible hope is not wishful thinking or uncertain

Scripture Resource: Romans 8:28, 37-39

desire. It is a confident and certain expectation of something good. It is called *hope* only because its object is still in the future, not because of any uncertainty.

There is a great deal of confused thinking about assurance of salvation. Some go to an unbiblical extreme, asserting that once a person is saved, he can be sure that he will never again be lost.

On the other hand, many sincere Christians deny the possibility of any assurance whatsoever. Instead of singing "Yes, my name's written there," they can only ask it as a question: "Is my name written there?" An elder in a local church exhibited this common doubt when he addressed his Sunday school class with these words: "If I get to heaven—and I emphasize the *if. . . ."*

Still others grant that assurance is possible, but they don't have it personally because they have a false idea of its basis. They think that assurance is based upon something they don't have or haven't yet experienced. Doubt and uncertainty still reign in their lives.

In this chapter we shall seek to expose false ideas and false bases of assurance. Then we shall explore the only proper foundation for Christian certainty, namely, the love and grace of God as evidenced in the work of Christ and as received via justification by faith at baptism.

I. Assurance and Predestination

The doctrine of eternal security or "once saved, always saved" began with a North African church leader named Augustine, who died in A.D. 430. It was originally part of a system or cluster of doctrines known to many people today as Calvinism.

Augustine began with the idea that everyone is totally depraved from birth. As a result no one is able to believe and respond to the gospel of his own free will. Thus God himself chooses who will believe and be saved. He does this choosing before the creation of the world. This is what is known as unconditional predestination or election. (It is unconditional because God does not ask us to meet any conditions for being chosen.) At the proper time, God opens the hearts of those whom He has predestined. He turns their wills and causes them to believe the gospel. (This is called "irresistible grace.")

In other words, God controls the process of salvation from beginning to end. Our wills have nothing to do with it. God overrides our wills and makes us believe. And *in the same way,* He continues to override our wills by preventing us from ever *losing* our faith and salvation. Hence, "once saved, always saved."

This whole system is based upon the false idea of total depravity. It is true that a sinner cannot do good works and live a life of obedience to God's law (Romans 8:7-8). But one thing is clear in the Bible: every sinner *can* decide to turn from sin and surrender himself to God, who *then* regenerates him and enables him to live in accordance with the law. God does not coerce; He invites: "Whoever is thirsty, let him come; and *whoever wishes,* let him take the free gift of the water of life" (Revelation 22:17).

This system also includes a false understanding of predestination. God does not predestine depraved sinners to become believers. He *does* predestine certain ones to *Heaven,* but only because He *foreknows* that they will freely accept His invitation and become believers by their own choice. Romans 8:29 makes it clear: "For those God *foreknew* he also predestined to be conformed to the likeness of his Son. . . ." (The "likeness of his Son" is the glorified, resurrected state we will share with Christ in Heaven.)

Thus God does not override man's will to bring him to salvation. Likewise, God does not override our wills to *keep* us saved. The Bible makes it plain that a believer will be saved only if he continues in his faith. See, for example, Colossians 1:23; Hebrews 3:6-14; 4:1, 11; 6:4-6.

A few denominations continue to hold the "once

saved, always saved" doctrine, while rejecting total depravity, unconditional election, and irresistible grace. In other words, they hold to a belief that makes sense only within a certain framework, though they have rightly rejected the framework itself. The next proper step is to reject "once saved, always saved" as well.

The Bible teaches assurance, but not an unconditional assurance that ignores man's will and violates his freedom of choice.

II. Assurance and Experience

A common idea today is that if you have had a certain kind of feeling or experience, you can know you are saved. The kind of experience may vary. For some, it would be a warm, tingly feeling experienced while praying. For others, it would be the ability to "speak in tongues."

Whatever the experience, the idea is the same. If you have had it or felt it or done it, then you are saved. Many also draw the opposite conclusion: if you have *not* had such an experience, then you are not saved.

We must insist, however, that this whole approach is wrong. In the first place, any subjective feeling is ambiguous. That is, it may be interpreted in a number of ways. How do we know that we are interpreting our feelings correctly? This is especially significant when we try to discern the origin or cause of any subjective feeling. How can we be sure that our "tongue-speaking" is not psychologically conditioned, or caused by demonic powers? This inherent ambiguity makes experience a poor basis for assurance.

Also, feelings and experiences are subject to frequent change. We may have a wonderful feeling today, and conclude that we are truly saved. But what if we have a tragic experience tomorrow, or wake up feeling rotten? Must we then conclude that we are *not* saved?

Finally, the Word of God has nowhere said that a particular subjective feeling or experience is a sure sign of personal salvation. Our assurance is tied to objective events, as we shall see below. The one who looks within himself will find no true basis for hope.

III. Assurance and Good Works

Perhaps the saddest approach is that which links assurance of salvation to a certain degree of personal goodness. Here a person is usually thinking in terms of being "good enough" to be saved. He is thinking in terms of law, not grace.

Incredibly, some may decide that they are indeed good enough to be saved, and may have a strong feeling of assurance. But such people are deceiving themselves, like the Pharisee in Jesus' parable (Luke 18:9-12).

Most people who base assurance on goodness draw a different conclusion, however. Most realize that we *are* sinners who do not deserve to be saved. Most recognize that even as Christians we still are not perfect. We fall short of our goal day after day. How then can we say that we are *saved?* Isn't this the height of pride and presumption? We just are not good enough. Hence, assurance is impossible in this life. One will know he is saved only after his works have been evaluated and approved on the judgment day.

What a sad yet common attitude among God's people! It is true that no one is good enough to deserve salvation. But under *grace* our salvation is not given to us because we deserve it or are good enough for it. Under grace, we are saved *even though* we are sinners. The sin is there, but it is covered by the blood of Christ. This is the ground of our hope.

In other words, it is an error for us to link our assurance to the particular degree of goodness or sanctification which we may have achieved at any point in life. Such an approach denies the fact that we are justified by faith. The real key to assurance is an awareness of just this fact: we are justified by faith, not by works of law (Romans 3:28).

IV. Assurance and God's Promises

Here is the question: if you were to die at this very moment, would you go to Heaven? Close your eyes and think about your answer. As you considered the question, what did you think of first? Yourself? Your own feelings, experiences, or goodness? No wonder you are filled with doubt and despair! All this ground is "sinking sand."

Or did your mind turn instead toward God? Did you remember His love, His promises, and His faithfulness? Did you thank Him for His grace, which is greater than all our sin? If so, then you were able to answer *yes* to the question. Here alone—in God, not in us—lies the basis for personal assurance.

Our assurance rests ultimately on God's promises. We are, literally, "standing on the promises of God." He has promised us that He loves us, that He has forgiven us, and that He will take us to Heaven. He has tied these promises to certain objective events so that we may grasp them and be sure of them.

There are three events especially in which God's promises are objectified and fulfilled. Whenever we are tempted to doubt our salvation, we should just recall these events.

First, there is the fact that *Christ died for our* sins. The death of Jesus is the ultimate proof that God loves us. "But God demonstrates his own love for us in this: While we were still sinners, Christ died for us" (Romans 5:8; see John 3:16).

When we are tempted to doubt whether God really loves us, we should remember Calvary, God's unbreakable guarantee that He is for us. "He who did not spare his own Son, but gave him up for us all—how will he not also, along with him, graciously give us all things?" (Romans 8:32) "Who shall separate us from the love of Christ? Shall trouble or hardship or persecution or famine or nakedness or danger or sword?" No! Nothing will "be able to separate us from the love of God that is in Christ Jesus our Lord" (Romans 8:35-39).

No matter what may happen, nothing can change the fact that Christ died for us. Why should we then doubt His love?

In Romans 5 Paul makes this assurance even more firm. He says that if God loved us so much while we were *sinners* that He gave his Son for us, will He not love us even *more,* now that we are reconciled to Him (verses 8, 9)? "For if, when we were God's *enemies,* we were reconciled to him through the death of his Son, how much *more,* having been reconciled, shall we be saved through his life!" (Romans 5:10).

The second event which confirms God's promises to us is the *resurrection of Jesus.* God promises to give us life: to raise us from spiritual death in baptism, and to raise our bodies at the Second Coming. Why are we able to believe this? Because God has promised, and because He demonstrates His ability and desire to do so in the resurrection of Jesus. See Colossians 2:12.

The third event which embodies God's promise is *our own baptism.* We know God loves us and can save us, because of the death and resurrection of Jesus. But how do we know that we personally have been saved? Because God has promised to do so in baptism, and God keeps His promises.

I know I am saved if I am forgiven or justified, since this means having all my guilt and punishment removed. I know I am justified if I am under the blood of Christ. And I know I came under Christ's blood in Christian baptism. I know because I trust in God's promises.

I may doubt my feelings. I may wonder about my experiences, especially after the passage of time. But I still have an objective reference point which I will not forget:

the time when I met God in baptism, and there received all that He promised to give me.

Christian hope rests on God's promises, not on our feelings. It rests on these works of God, not upon our works. Let our minds then rest upon God's strength and faithfulness, not upon our own weakness and fickleness. "Let us hold unswervingly to the hope we profess, for he who promised is faithful" (Hebrews 10:23).

Chapter 10

Does God Play Favorites?

Is God prejudiced?

Does God treat certain people as His "teacher's pets"?

Does God have His "favorites" among all the peoples of the world?

The answer to such questions is a resounding "No!" A basic principle of the Bible is that "God does not show favoritism" (Romans 2:11). Or as other translations put it, "For there is no respect of persons with God" (KJV).

In light of this clear teaching, why do we speak of the Jewish nation as "God's chosen people"? How are we to understand the special treatment which God has accorded the Jews in times past? Many Christians even believe that God will once again elevate the Jews to a place of privilege in connection with Christ's return. How could any of this be so, if God does not show favoritism?

In this chapter we shall try to resolve these apparent conflicts. We shall explore the question of God's

Scripture Resource: Romans 10:5-13; 11:33-36

purpose for the Jewish nation in relation to His overall purpose of grace.

I. Israel's Separation

How Odd of God to Choose the Jews, an unknown author once reflected in the title of a book.

Indeed, God *did* choose the Jews and bring them into a unique relation with himself. As Deuteronomy 7:6 says, "For thou art an holy people unto the Lord thy God: the Lord thy God hath chosen thee to be a special people unto himself, above all people that are upon the face of the earth" (KJV).

A. Her Purpose

Why did God do this? The answer lies in God's purpose for the world in general. On the very day when sin entered the human race, God had announced His plan to send a Savior (Genesis 3:15). But before the Savior could enter history and accomplish His work, preparations had to be made. The key element in the plan was the choosing of a single nation as the *means* of the Redeemer's entry into the world. That nation was Israel.

It is extremely important to recognize that Israel's exclusiveness was not an end in itself. It was rather a *temporary expedient,* merely a means to a much greater end: the first coming of Christ.

This larger purpose of grace is clearly seen in God's first step toward making the Jews a separate people, namely, the call of Abraham. God promised to make of Abraham "a great nation," but His climactic promise was this: "And in thee shall *all* families of the earth be blessed" (Genesis 12:2-3, KJV; see Genesis 26:4). The rest of the Old Testament tells about God's dealings with the people He had selected for carrying out His purpose.

B. Her Preparation

Exactly why was it necessary to concentrate upon just

one nation? The key word is *preparation.* Consider the analogy of preparing a plot of land before sowing seeds for a crop. In like manner God had to plow and cultivate and prepare a selected field, so that it would be ready to receive the blessed Seed of Abraham when He came.

A major element in the preparation was the giving of special revelation. God would not send the Redeemer unannounced, unexplained, and unexpected. The Jewish nation served as the necessary receptacle for this revelation. Her prophets received and recorded God's own word, which explained His purpose of grace. As the people read and preserved these wonderful prophecies, they developed a strong sense of expectation and hope. When Jesus came, at least a remnant was ready for Him.

C. Her Privilege

So the exclusiveness of the Jews was only a temporary expedient in God's plan to show mercy upon all. Does this detract from their honor and importance in performing this service? Not at all. Considered as a single nation, their privilege has been unmatched throughout history.

"First of all," says Paul, "they have been entrusted with the very words of God" (Romans 3:2). Further, "Theirs is the adoption as sons; theirs the divine glory, the covenants, the receiving of the law, the temple worship and the promises." And grandest of all, "from them is traced the human ancestry of Christ, who is God over all, forever praised! Amen" (Romans 9:4-5).

What other nation in history can ever come close to the honor and privileges bestowed upon the Jews? Not one!

II. Israel's Rejection

Once their purpose of bringing the world's Savior into history had been accomplished, it might seem that the Jews were then just cast aside like an old shoe. This may appear to be the case especially since God's primary attention is now focused on the church. "I ask then, Did

God reject his people?" Paul answers his own question: "By no means!" (Romans 11:1).

A. The Addition of the Gentiles

The fact is that God had never intended for Israel to *remain* a separate nation once her primary purpose had been fulfilled. Nor, in fact, did He simply intend to *replace* her, with some other nation being put in the spotlight of God's affection. God's plan was and always had been to take the believing remnant (Romans 11:5), the true Israelites (Romans 2:28-29), and use them as the foundation and core for a *new* Israel. The new Israel would include all heart-believers, including Jews and Gentiles.

This plan was accomplished. The new Israel was begun on the Day of Pentecost following the resurrection and ascension of Jesus. It is called *the church.*

The eventual inclusion of the Gentiles was part of God's basic plan from the beginning. The promise to Abraham shows this (Genesis 12:3). Paul comments on this promise: "The Scripture foresaw that God would justify the Gentiles by faith, and announced the gospel in advance to Abraham: 'All nations will be blessed in you' " (Galatians 3:8; see 3:14). Of the new Israel Isaiah said, "And the Gentiles shall come to thy light" (Isaiah 60:3). As Joel 2:32 prophesied, "Whosoever shall call on the name of the Lord shall be delivered" (KJV). This ingathering of the Gentiles is a basic message of the prophets.

The Jews' final privilege was to form the root of the new Israel. Paul uses the analogy of an olive tree in Romans 11:16-24. Israel was like a domestic olive tree, which had been carefully tended for centuries. But at the proper time God grafted new branches onto the old tree—wild olive branches, representing the Gentiles.

God had no intention of excluding Israel. He wanted to retain them as the natural branches, and *add* the Gentiles, making one body in which "there is no difference between Jew and Gentile" (Romans 10:12).

B. The Unbelief of the Jews

Why is it, then, that after the earliest days the Jews never had a very prominent place in the church? It is not because God has rejected them. It is rather because *they have rejected God.* In unbelief the bulk of the nation has rejected God's gospel of grace.

Paul declares that his own Jewish brethren would not accept salvation as a free gift through faith. They persisted instead in the false notion that they could be saved by their works (Romans 9:31-33). As Paul put it, "They disregarded the righteousness that comes from God and sought to establish their own" (Romans 10:3).

Because God's righteousness can be received only by faith, God had no choice but to exclude from His new Israel every Jew who refused to believe. The unbelieving branches were simply broken off their own tree (Romans 11:17) because of their unbelief (11:20).

This was not true of every Jew, of course. In fact, the earliest church was made up exclusively of Jews, and it took a special sign from God just to convince even the apostles that God was now ready to receive the Gentiles also (Acts 10:9-48). These believing Jews were the "remnant chosen by grace" (Romans 11:5).

What is significant in this is that God is no longer treating the Jews as a nation, but as individuals. Those who believe are included in the new Israel; those who refuse to believe are excluded by their own choice.

III. The New Israel: Whosoever Will

In God's new Israel, the church, His original purpose is fulfilled. All are joined together in a unity transcending nationality or race. The gospel goes out to all indiscriminately: "For *whosoever* shall call upon the name of the Lord shall be saved" (Romans 10:13, KJV). Those who accept the offer are treated equally: "There is neither Jew nor Greek, slave nor free, male nor female, for you are all one in Christ Jesus" (Galatians 3:28).

This was a lesson which the earliest church had difficulty learning. Being converted Jews, they could not believe that God also wanted Gentiles to join them in one body. But through a series of revelations (Acts 10:9-33) the Lord persuaded Peter that this was indeed His will. "Peter answered, 'I now realize how true it is that God does not show favoritism but accepts men from every nation who fear him and do what is right' " (Acts 10:34-35).

A. A Plan for the Jews?

Many people believe that God still has a special role for the Jews as a nation. The restoration of the Jews to Palestine, they believe, is but the prelude to their exaltation to prominence in a great kingdom Christ will establish on earth when He returns.

This belief is unfounded, however, being based upon a faulty understanding of prophecy. Some try to apply biblical prophecies concerning the restoration of the Jews from Babylonian captivity around 536 B.C. to present-day events in Palestine. Prophecies referring to the new Israel, which is a spiritual kingdom, are taken to refer to a restored physical kingdom of the Jews.

The fact is that God's glorious purpose for the Jews as a nation was fulfilled in Christ's first coming. (See, for instance, Acts 13:32-33.) The Jewish nation as such no longer has a place in God's plan.

But this does not mean that God has no plan at all for the Jews. He does indeed have such a plan, not for the nation as a whole, but for any individual Jew who will accept the gospel of grace. That plan is to include them in the new Israel, the church.

Using the figure of the olive tree, Paul says, "And if they do not persist in unbelief, they will be grafted in, for God is able to graft them in again. After all, if you were cut out of an olive tree that is wild by nature, and contrary to nature were grafted into a cultivated olive tree, how much more readily will these, the natural branches, be grafted into their own olive tree?'' (Romans 11:23-24).

"And so all Israel will be saved," says Paul (Romans 11:26). the word *so* here means "thus, in this manner." *This* is God's plan for the Jews: to save them in the same way that anyone else is saved, by adding them to the church.

"All Israel" in Romans 11:26 may mean all of the new or spiritual Israel, or it may mean all Jews who are *truly* Jews through heart-belief in Jesus Christ (Romans 2:28-29; 10:9; 11:5).

B. Mercy for All

The church of Christ can be true to her nature only by offering the gospel to all peoples and races indiscriminately. God's purpose is fulfilled only when all heart-believers are united in Christ into an undivided body.

If God does not show favoritism, then certainly His church must not!

Christ has destroyed once for all times the wall which divided Jews from Gentiles (Ephesians 2:14). There are many other kinds of walls which separate us from one another in this present evil age: racism, denominationalism, social snobbishness, political and ideological warfare, suspicion, jealousy. Christ the great Wall-Destroyer can tear these down, too!

This will not occur on a universal basis, since such walls are erected by sinful hearts and will not be torn down unless the hearts are changed. But for any who surrender to Christ for forgiveness and regeneration, all barriers to brotherhood are demolished. In Christ, in His church, all are one.

Every local congregation of Christ's church should examine itself in light of God's purpose to have mercy upon all. Let there "be no divisions among you" (1 Corinthians 1:10)! May racial prejudice, snobbish cliques, and social compartments be unknown among God's people! How else can we be true to the gospel?

Chapter 11

Mercy: Grace in Action

"Therefore, I urge you, brothers, in view of God's mercy, to offer yourselves as living sacrifices, holy and pleasing to God—which is your spiritual worship" (Romans 12:1).

"In view of God's mercy"—after all, from what other perspective could a Christian view his life and his responsibilities? We have experienced God's mercy in all its depth and riches. We who were God's own enemies, we who were ungodly and undeserving—we have been reconciled to God by the death of His own dear Son. What mercy! What grace!

In view of the fact that we have been reconciled, we ought to live the reconciled life. In view of our experience of God's love, we ought to live a life of love. In view of our being forgiven, we ought to forgive. "In view of God's mercy," we ought always to be merciful.

In other words, our daily lives ought to reflect the very nature and character of the grace and mercy which God

Scripture Resource: Romans 12:3-18

has showed to us. The very attitudes that the merciful God has exhibited toward us are the attitudes that we must have toward our fellow man.

The reconciled life may well be best exemplified by the characteristic of *mercy*. Jesus said, "Blessed are the merciful, for they will be shown mercy" (Matthew 5:7). How can we be merciful? How can we who have seen the mercy of God show mercy to others? These are the questions we seek to answer in this chapter.

I. Mercy: Moved by Misery

Compassion is a form of mercy. Many hospitals are named "Mercy Hospital," suggesting compassion for the sick and suffering. Charity is another channel of mercy; thus a beggar cries, "Have mercy on a poor man." Clemency to criminals may be shown if a jury recommends mercy.

These examples of the way we use the word *mercy* show us that mercy is a concern for the needs of others. To be merciful is to be *moved by misery*.

There is much misery in the world; hence there is a constant opportunity to show mercy. Physical miseries are suffered by the poor, the hungry, the starving, the diseased, the addicted, and the oppressed. Spiritual miseries are even more abundant. Multitudes are burdened with guilt and the fear of death. They are plagued by feelings of loneliness, emptiness, and meaninglessness.

The Christian must be moved with compassion by this misery, as Jesus was by the misery around Him (Matthew 9:36; 14:14). Mercy and indifference are incompatible. Real Christian love *(agape)* is most precisely defined as concern, compassion, and care. "Love," says Paul, "must be sincere" (Romans 12:9). How can it be sincere if the awareness of misery does not fill us with inner pain and sympathetic suffering? How can it be sincere if we are not moved to try to relieve the misery?

We must strive to develop a real tenderheartedness in

reference to the sufferings of others. We must really care—to the point of tears. We must be able, as Paul says, to "mourn with those who mourn" (Romans 12:15). We must be *moved* by misery.

This is mercy, and such mercy is what distinguishes the Christian from the world. It is a peculiarly Christian virtue. Before Christianity revolutionized the world, mercy was practically unknown. Institutions of mercy today, even though secularized, are the product of Christian teaching about mercy.

The Christian, as a truly merciful person, is moved by *all kinds* of misery. Today's social activists are guilty of a one-sided concentration on physical and social misery. They usually ignore spiritual needs and miseries, which are actually more important because they are the source of other misery.

On the other hand, many of us may be guilty of a one-sidedness in the other direction. We concentrate on spiritual suffering and feel little need to concern ourselves with physical misery. Could it be that the social activists are just filling a vacuum left by the church?

As Christians we must reassert our duty to be merciful. Our primary responsibility is benevolence toward our fellow Christians: "Share with God's people who are in need. Practice hospitality" (Romans 12:13). But mercy goes beyond the borders of the church: "If your enemy is hungry, feed him; if he is thirsty, give him something to drink" (Romans 12:20).

A local congregation can find ways to show mercy, to relieve misery both in and out of its own neighborhood. Christians can choose careers of mercy, such as counseling, medicine, nursing, the ministry, or social work.

Let us remember, however, that *spiritual* misery is the most serious and must be the Christian's and the church's primary concern. Helping sinners to experience the mercy of God is our ultimate goal and the best expression of our own mercy for them.

II. Mercy: Free to Forgive

Mercy in its keenest form is forgiveness, showing compassion and kindness to someone who has wronged us. A merciful heart is able to put aside all thoughts of retaliation and sincerely forgive the wrongdoer.

We have this commandment: "Bless those who persecute you; bless and do not curse" (Romans 12:14). How can we do less, when we remember that we have been forgiven by the God against whom we sinned? "Be kind and compassionate to one another, forgiving each other, just as in Christ God forgave you" (Ephesians 4:32).

The Christian does not live by the "eye-for-an-eye" principle. That is the principle of justice; and it is to be applied by the lawcourts, not by the individual. Jesus teaches us, "Do not resist an evil person. If someone strikes you on the right cheek, turn to him the other also" (Matthew 5:39). As Paul puts it, "Do not repay anyone evil for evil. . . . Do not take revenge, my friends, but leave room for God's wrath, for it is written: 'It is mine to avenge, I will repay,' says the Lord" (Romans 12:17, 19). (One way that God exercises His vengeance is through the civil authorities; see Romans 13:1-4.)

We are to hold no grudges, seek no revenge; we must not desire to "get even" or to see the offender suffer unjustly.

An important Christian teaching is that only the merciful will obtain mercy. That is, those who do not forgive will not be forgiven. We should pray for forgiveness, says Jesus, only after we have forgiven others (Matthew 6:12). "For if you forgive men when they sin against you, your heavenly Father will also forgive you. But if you do not forgive men their sins, your Father will not forgive your sins" (Matthew 6:14-15).

James says that "judgment without mercy will be shown to anyone who has not been merciful" (James 2:13). Jesus' parable of the unmerciful servant (Matthew

18:21-35) makes this point with chilling clarity.

Does this seem too harsh? Does this seem to be contrary to the very principle of grace and mercy? Not when we remember that mercy and forgiveness are what Christianity is all about. It is *the way of the cross.* Not to forgive even the cruelest insult is so contrary to the very nature of Christianity, that one cannot be a Christian if he has an unforgiving spirit. One who persists in an unforgiving spirit has missed the whole point of the cross. A man who can't forgive does not know what it means to be forgiven.

A man once said to John Wesley, "I never forgive." Wesley answered, "Then I hope, sir, that you never sin."

The ultimate test of mercy, then, is always to be free and ready to forgive anyone who has wronged you. Are you merciful? Or is your spirit still ensnared and enshrouded with the bonds of retaliation and revenge? Do you always feel you have to get even with someone who insults or injures you? Or is your spirit free from this enslaving burden? Are you free to forgive?

The merciful truly are blessed. "The merciful man doeth good to his own soul: but he that is cruel troubleth his own flesh" (Proverbs 11:17).

III. Mercy: Generous Beyond Justice

It isn't easy to develop a merciful heart. So often we see someone in real misery and exclaim, "It serves him right. He brought it on himself. He deserves it. It's only fair." And perhaps that is true. We may be referring to an alcoholic, or to an unmarried expectant mother, or to a drug addict.

How often does someone wrong us, and we hesitate to forgive him and treat him with kindness? "He doesn't deserve it," we say. And probably he doesn't.

In other words, most of us have a very keen sense of *justice.* We know what is right, what is fair. This is one reason why it is so easy to get hooked on comic strips, soap operas, western movies, or even TV wrestling.

These usually involve villains, and we want to see the bad guys "get what's coming to them."

Our sense of justice is strongest when we ourselves have been wronged, when our "rights" have been violated. We demand justice! We will have our rights! We will make the offender pay! So we proceed to attack him, to humiliate him, or to demand an apology. "Turn about is *fair* play!" It is only *just.*

It is true: it may "serve an addict right" to suffer withdrawal pains. True: he brought it on himself, and he deserves it. True: a scoundrel doesn't deserve our forgiveness. True: turn about is fair play.

But whoever said that a Christian is supposed to be only *fair?* Whoever said we are supposed to treat people only as they deserve? Following the example and teaching of Jesus, the Christian must be *more* than fair. We must be generous *beyond* justice. This is mercy. This is grace in action.

We have no right to keep talking about our rights. We must forgive. Sure, he doesn't deserve it—but that's what it's all about! That's what mercy *is.* "Turn about is *fair* play," but kindness and forgiveness are the *merciful* way, the Christian way.

IV. Mercy: Guided by God

Our question now can only be "How?" How can we achieve this disposition or attitude of mercifulness? It would almost seem to be beyond human ability!

Indeed, it *is* beyond the ability of a sinful person to be merciful. We can attain this goal only when we let ourselves be guided by God. We can be merciful only when we follow God's example by God's power.

"Be merciful, just as your Father is merciful," says Jesus (Luke 6:36). Only God, "who is rich in mercy" (Ephesians 2:4), can be our standard. We must not let the world tell us how to act or even define mercy for us. The norm can only be God and His word.

The norm is truly a lofty one, and impossible to reach if one is outside of Christ. But a Christian *can* learn to be merciful, not by his own strength but by the power of the Holy Spirit who dwells within him (Ephesians 3:16; Philippians 2:13).

Let those who have been reconciled to God use this power, be merciful even to enemies, and show the unbelieving world what a beautiful thing the reconciled life can be.

Chapter 12

Don't Throw Stones

"I don't like *doctrinal* sermons. Give us something *practical.*" Every preacher hears this well-meant suggestion occasionally. The chapters in this book may be criticized by some as being too heavy on the doctrinal side.

A lesson which every Christian must learn, however, is that there is nothing more practical than doctrine. After all, doctrine is nothing more than teaching, i.e., what is taught and what is believed to be true. This is all-important, because what a man believes to be true determines everything else he does. Right doctrine thus is a prerequisite to right action.

No wonder the early Christians devoted themselves first of all to the apostles' doctrine (Acts 2:42). No wonder the Scriptures' primary value is its doctrine (2 Timothy 3:16).

The books of Romans and Galatians, which have formed the basis for this series of studies, are good

---

Scripture Resource: Romans 14:10-23

examples of this. They are solidly doctrinal books. But at the same time, they are very practical. Their focal point, the doctrine of justification by faith, lays the necessary foundation for every aspect of our relationship to God and for all our relationships to one another.

It is not surprising, then, that the book of Romans, especially in the latter chapters, has much to say about Christian love. What other response is possible by one who knows he has been saved by grace? Grace makes all other motivating factors obsolete. Those who are saved by grace will walk in love.

In this chapter we shall examine some aspects of neighbor-love as taught in the book of Romans.

I. Love Does No Harm

The first characteristic of love is found in this statement: "Love does no harm to its neighbor" (Romans 13:10). If we love another person, in no way do we want to see that person hurt or harmed. An old saying is that "you always hurt the one you love." The point, of course, is that nobody really *wants* to hurt someone he loves, but because of life's ironies, our actions often hurt a loved one unintentionally. Real love, however, will do everything possible to avoid such harm.

This is why so many of God's commandments are couched in negative terms. The commandments, after all, are merely the specific application of the general law of love. If a person loves his neighbor, he will not harm him by stealing from him, by lying to him, or by killing him. Thus it is quite proper for the commands to tell us what *not* to do. When one does not do such things, he is to that extent fulfilling the law of love. (See Romans 13:8-10.)

A. Weak or Strong?

A specific application of this principle is found in Romans 14. Paul admonishes a Christian not to harm his brother by causing him to sin against his conscience. "Therefore, let us stop passing judgment on one another. Instead, make up your mind not to put any stumbling block or obstacle in your brother's way" (Romans 14:13). Even if you are doing something that is perfectly harmless in itself, if your Christian brother believes it is wrong but is led to do it by your example, "you are no longer acting in love" (Romans 14:15).

Here the subject has to do with things or activities which are not wrong in God's sight, and with the weak and strong approaches to such things. A Christian who is still weak in faith and who lacks proper understanding may feel that a certain harmless activity is quite sinful. If so, he should not engage in that activity, since he would be going against his conscience and thus committing a sin (Romans 14:14, 23; 1 Corinthians 8:7).

A strong Christian, however, is one who knows when something is harmless and who can therefore engage in it without sin. Of course, this does not refer to anything that is actually condemned by God's Word, but to things about which the Bible does not speak either directly or by implication.

In New Testament writings the main example of such an activity is eating meat offered to idols. In ancient butcher shops a main source of supply for fresh meat was the local pagan temple. Animals would be killed as sacrifices to various idols, then sold in the markets for ordinary consumption. Individual Christians could not agree concerning the rightness or wrongness of eating such meat. Those who considered it sinful preferred to eat no meat at all rather than to risk eating what could be to their minds polluted.

Paul makes it clear that eating such meat is perfectly harmless (1 Corinthians 8:4-6; 10:25-27). One who is strong in faith knows this. Sin is incurred by those who offer the animal to an idol, not by those who eat the meat as a gift from God.

B. Liberty or Love?

But this is not the end of the problem. " 'Everything is permissible,' " says Paul, "but not everything is beneficial" and constructive (1 Corinthians 10:23). Even though I may be free to eat meat sacrificed to idols, someone weaker than I may be led into sin thereby. If he sees me eating such meat, and is led to indulge in it against his conscience, he has sinned (1 Corinthians 8:9-12).

What is the answer? For one who *loves* his neighbor, it is very simple. It is against love to cause a brother to stumble. Therefore if my eating meat causes him to stumble, it is wrong for me to eat meat. Love does no harm! Thus Paul says, "If your brother is distressed because of what you eat, you are no longer acting in love. Do not by your eating destroy your brother for whom Christ died" (Romans 14:15).

"It is better," he says, "not to eat meat or drink wine or to do anything else that will cause your brother to fall" (Romans 14:21; see 1 Corinthians 8:13). The law of liberty gives way to the law of love.

This principle must be applied diligently wherever necessary. It may involve playing cards or billiards, or going to the movies, or working on Sunday afternoon. It may involve listening to certain types of music or watching certain programs on television. Whatever it is, we must always be aware of the effects our actions have on others. We must be willing to forego our liberties (our "rights") if exercising them would lead a weaker brother into sin.

C. Judgment or Acceptance?

Let us note that the actual giving up of such activities is necessary only if we are causing others to stumble thereby, namely, only if they are actually tempted to *do* these things and sin in their hearts. We need not give up something which merely "offends" a brother, in the sense that he just doesn't like it or approve of it and is repelled by it. (There is some confusion here because our older translations use the word *offend,* which in earlier days actually meant "to cause to stumble.")

Along this line Paul says that if there is disagreement among brethren over such matters of opinion, let each respect the views of others and not be judgmental. (See Romans 14:1-13.)

The guiding principle in all such matters is still this: Love does no harm.

II. Love Helps Others Grow

Love is not satisfied merely with doing no harm to others. It also seeks to express itself positively by helping others to grow in their faith and knowledge. We should "make every effort to do what leads to peace and to mutual edification" (Romans 14:19). "Each of us should please his neighbor for his good, to *build him up*" (Romans 15:2).

If we know of "weaker brothers" whose Christian lives are fragile and strained because of faulty understanding of Scripture, let us study with them and encourage them in a proper knowledge of God and His world. If we have weaker brothers who are having difficulty overcoming sin, let us offer ourselves to be of service in any way possible. "We who are strong ought to bear with the failings of the weak" (Romans 15:1).

Whatever gift we have received from the Holy Spirit, we should put it to use to help the other members of Christ's body to grow. Paul compares the church to a body, pointing out that each of us is mutually dependent on all other members. (See Romans 12:4, 5.)

The spiritual gifts that are mentioned in Romans 12:6-8 are gifts which, when exercised, will build up our brothers and sisters in the Lord. Some early Christians could prophesy, thus enriching the hearts of all by bringing them messages from the Lord. Others have less spectacular but still indispensable gifts, such as teaching and leading and encouraging. Some are especially tenderhearted and are able to show mercy and compassion when needed most. Some may be unusually blessed with earthly treasures and have the gift of giving. By supporting such things as ministerial training and world-wide evangelism, they render a vital ministry and help to build up the whole body of Christ.

III. Love Puts Others First

Love reaches its climax when one is able to put the needs and desires of others above his own. Jesus said, "Love your neighbor as yourself" (Matthew 22:39). That is, have the same *kind* of love for your neighbor as for yourself.

Jesus is not saying that we should have the same *amount* of love for others as for ourselves. In fact, His word teaches that we should have more love for others than for self. The greatest love of all is when one can lay down his very life for his friends (John 15:13).

This must be the way we love from day to day. It may not necessarily require giving up our lives, but it may definitely require us to give up *something* for our neighbor's good. Referring to the problem about meat offered to idols, Paul said he was perfectly willing to give up eating meat if that was harming anyone (1 Corinthians 8:13). What are we willing to give up for the sake of our neighbors and brethren?

This is not a matter of choice if our love is sincere. We are to put others first. "Be devoted to one another in brotherly love. Honor one another above yourselves" (Romans 12:10). We are "not to please ourselves," but "each of us should please his neighbor for *his* good." Even Christ did not please himself (Romans 15:1-3).

In the words of John, "Dear children, let us not love with words or tongue but with actions and in truth" (1 John 3:18). Let us walk in love—doing no harm, helping others grow, and putting others first.

Chapter 13

I.O.U.

Most of us know only too well what it means to be in debt. We know that it means to be obligated to another person in some way. Most commonly the debt is a financial one; we obligate ourselves to pay a certain amount of money to someone.

There is, however, another kind of debt. We may call it a moral debt, a moral obligation. If someone befriends us with an act of great kindness, we say that we owe him a debt of gratitude. If a man commits a crime, he goes to prison to pay his debt to society. When we make a promise, we have a moral obligation to keep our word. Parents are morally obligated to support their children; children are morally obligated to obey their parents.

It is in this second sense, the sense of moral obligation, that the Bible teaches us to say, "We are debtors." We are debtors both to God and to our fellow men.

This fact is emphasized by the New Testament's

Scripture Resource: Romans 1:16; 15:8-21
This chapter is reprinted with permission from Standard Lesson Commentary 1974-75, pp. 119, 120.

frequent use of words which have to do with being in debt. First there is the noun *opheile,* which means "debt, obligation, duty." Second there is the noun *opheiletes,* meaning "a debtor, one who is under a certain obligation." Finally we have the verb *opheilein,* which means "to be under obligation, to owe a debt." Most often this last word is translated "ought."

By paying close attention to the use of these words in the New Testament, we shall see here that we are debtors in three different ways: as creatures, as sinners, and as Christians.

I. We Creatures Are Debtors

Our basic debt to God is a debt of obedience. We owe it to God to obey His every commandment. This is true because God is the sovereign Creator of all that exists, including human beings.

Psalm 24:1, 2 says,

> The earth is the Lord's, and the fulness thereof; the world, and they that dwell therein.
>
> For he hath founded it upon the seas, and established it upon the floods (KJV).

Here we are told that God is the owner of everything because He has created it. Both the earth and "they that dwell therein" are the Lord's. As our owner, God has complete lordship over us; we owe Him total submission. We owe Him perfect obedience to all His commandments.

Jesus states this point explicitly in the parable of the unprofitable servant (Luke 17:7-10). Here He tells us that even if we do *all* the things commanded of us, we should expect no special recognition or rewards. Why? Because "we have only done our duty" (v. 10). The word used here is *opheilein;* literally Jesus is saying, "We have done that which we were indebted to do." When we give perfect obedience, we pay to God the debt we owe Him as His creatures.

II. We Sinners Are Debtors

What happens when we do not pay our debt of obedience? What happens when we sin? In this case we increase our indebtedness; we add another debt to our account.

But it is not simply a matter of adding to our original debt as creatures. Sin places us under a *different kind* of debt. Because we have sinned and have broken God's law, we are obligated to *pay the penalty.* As a criminal must pay his "debt to society," so must the sinner pay his debt to the Holy Lawgiver. We as sinners owe to God the debt of eternal punishment.

The Bible speaks of sin as a debt. In the model prayer Jesus teaches us to pray, "Forgive us our debts, as we also have forgiven our debtors" (Matthew 6:12). Jesus does not say, "Forgive us our trespasses;" He uses the word *debts.*

Likewise in Luke 13:4, 5 Jesus speaks of eighteen men who died in an accident, "Think ye that they were sinners above all men that dwelt in Jerusalem? I tell you, Nay; but, except ye repent, ye shall all likewise perish" (KJV). The word translated *sinners* here literally means *debtors.*

Jesus tells two parables which describe our predicament as sinners as being in debt. One is the parable of the forgiven debtors (Luke 7:41, 42); the other is the parable of the unforgiving servant (Matthew 18:21-35). The latter parable especially shows that the sinner must pay all that he owes (verse 34), and what he owes is eternal punishment in hell.

Few things are more depressing than being deep in debt with little prospect of relief. This is how we as sinners should feel when we realize that we are debtors and that *God will extract His payment.* No feeling of despair can match that which accompanies the debt of sin.

But here is where the gospel becomes good news indeed. The voice of Calvary cries out to hopeless hearts, "Jesus paid it all!" The first and primary datum of the gospel is just this, that "Christ died for our sins" (1 Corinthians 15:1-3). What this means specifically is that on the cross Jesus was suffering the penalty for *our* sins. He paid the debt of punishment for us.

This is one of the basic aspects of Christ's work as Redeemer. To redeem literally means "to set free by paying a price." Jesus paid the ransom-price to set us free from our debt. As he said, "Even so the Son of man came . . . to give his life a ransom for many" (Matthew 20:28; KJV).

Paul puts it this way: "For there is one God and one mediator between God and men, the man Christ Jesus, who gave himself as a ransom for all . . ." (1 Timothy 2:5, 6). He also says, "Christ redeemed us from the curse of the law by becoming a curse for us . . ." (Galatians 3:13). As the song-writer has said it, "On the cross he sealed my pardon—paid the debt and made me free."

There is a difference between our debt of obedience as creatures and our debt of punishment as sinners. Because we have free will, we can choose whether we will pay the first debt or not. Of course, to choose not to meet our obligation of obedience is sin; but nevertheless it is a matter of choice.

This is not the case, however, with regard to the debt of punishment. It is a debt which *must* be paid. The holiness of God demands it. But God has still left us a choice—the most blessed choice a sinner has. We can choose to pay the debt of punishment ourselves in hell forever, or we can choose to let Christ pay it for us. Indeed, Jesus has already deposited the full ransom-price in the Bank of Calvary; it is applied to our account when we meet Him by faith in baptism.

Let us praise God for Christ our Redeemer. It is a wonderful thing to be able to pray to God in complete confidence, "Forgive us our debts" (Matthew 6:12), knowing that Jesus has paid the price for us.

III. We Christians Are Debtors

One of our hymns says, "Jesus paid it all; all to him I owe." What did Jesus pay? He paid the debt of punishment we owe. But this does not mean that we are free from obligation. Indeed, as Christians, we now owe the greatest debt of all: the debt of love and gratitude. Truly, "All to him I owe."

If we are Christians, we owe it to Jesus to walk as He walked. 1 John 2:6 (KJV) says, "He that saith he abideth in him ought himself so to walk, even as he walked." Here the word *ought* is *opheilein:* we owe it to him to live the Christian life.

Romans 8:12 (KJV) says that "we are debtors, not to the flesh, to live after the flesh." The implied contrast is that we are debtors to live after the Spirit, to be "led by the Spirit of God" (verse 14).

The longer we are Christians, the greater is our obligation to grow in grace and knowledge. Hebrews 5:12 says that we owe it to Him (we *ought)* to be teachers of the Word of God. If we have been Christians we have the same obligation to God that we do as creatures, namely, we owe Him perfect obedience to all His commandments. But it is not the same kind of debt. We are no longer just creatures; we are new creatures (2 Corinthians 5:17). What obligates us now is not just creation, but redemption as well.

To put it another way, the Christian renders obedience to God not because of law, but because of grace. We obey not just because we feel we *have* to; we serve our Savior because we *want* to. In light of all He has done for us, how can we do less? "Oh to grace how great a debtor daily I'm constrained to be!"

Christian obedience and Christian good works must not, however, be considered as a way of "paying God back" for what He has done for us. They are rather the only proper way of saying "Thank you" to the one who paid our debt of punishment. Under grace, the debt of obedience becomes a debt of gratitude.

There is another important difference in our status as debtors under grace. We are debtors not only to God, but to our fellow men as well. Loving gratitude to our Redeemer constrains us to fulfil certain obligations toward others.

This principle is stated in its most basic form in John 4:11, which says, "Dear friends, since God so loved us, we also ought to love one another." Again the word *ought* is *opheilein:* we are debtors to love one another. Romans 13:8 exhorts explicitly, "Let no debt remain outstanding, except the continuing debt to love one another."

In what specific ways can we discharge our debt to one another? One way is to help those who are weaker and less fortunate than we are. "We who are strong ought— are under obligation—to bear with the failings of the weak, and not to please ourselves" (Romans 15:1). Lending a hand to help (or an arm to lean on, or a shoulder to cry on) is not a matter of choice; it is a debt we owe.

Jesus himself placed us under this obligation even before His blood washed away our debt of punishment on Calvary. In the upper room on the night before His crucifixion, He set the example of humble service when He washed the disciples' feet. Then He said, "Now that I, your Lord and Teacher, have washed your feet, you also should *(opheilein)* wash one another's feet" (John 13:14).

One of the most pressing debts which the Christian owes is his debt to the unsaved. God has saved us; He has done so freely by His grace and therefore does not expect us to "pay Him back." But He does expect the love of Christ to constrain us to act as His ambassadors and proclaim His reconciliation to those yet unsaved (2 Corinthians 5:14-20).

This is the debt which drove the Apostle Paul from country to country preaching Christ. As he said, "I am debtor both to the Greeks, and to the Barbarians; both to the wise, and to the unwise. So, as much as in me is, I am ready to preach . . ." (Romans 1:14, 15a; KJV).

Suppose that you as a lawyer received word that a distant relative of yours had died and bequeathed to you and to your brothers and sisters one million dollars each. You would not only rejoice for yourself, but you would be under a moral obligation to tell your brothers and sisters the good news. Likewise we as Christians, who already enjoy the riches of grace, are debtors to the world to tell them how Christ died for them, too.

Most of us are quite responsible when it comes to meeting our debts to the bank or to the department store or to the doctor. We would not seriously consider trying to get out of meeting such obligations. Likewise, it is time for us to take the debts of the Christian life seriously. After all, these are the largest and most important debts we owe. They are the debts of gratitude to the eternal God for the redemption that is in Christ Jesus. May we heed the words of our Lord and "render . . . unto God the things that are God's" (Matthew 22:21; KJV).